THE CIVIL RIGHTS MOVEMENT

A PHOTOGRAPHIC HISTORY, 1954–68

THE CIVIL RIGHTS MOVEMENT
A PHOTOGRAPHIC HISTORY, 1954–68

Steven Kasher
Foreword by Myrlie Evers-Williams

ABBEVILLE PRESS | PUBLISHERS | NEW YORK | LONDON | PARIS

CONTENTS

Myrlie Evers-Williams

My husband lay dying in a pool of blood on the doorstep of our home in Jackson, Mississippi. His body had been toppled by a cowardly assassin's bullet and left for the world—and his children—to see. I can still see Medgar's handsome features distorted in excruciating pain as he succumbed to death's premature call. It is this distinct memory of his final hours during that June day in 1963 that has haunted me as I have looked back over this book's often scathing yet also inspiriting images.

I don't remember the details of his funeral. That widely publicized photo of a tearstained young woman mourning the death of her first love could not have been me. I was too inexperienced to have been a widow. And my husband was too peace-loving to have been a casualty of war.

Just days before Medgar's death, he had remarked to a reporter: "If I die, it will be in a good cause. I've been fighting for America just as much as soldiers in Vietnam." I wonder about the images that my husband must have carried within him on his quest for equality. How emotionally draining it must have been on his spirit to bear in mind the unrecognizable portrait of the battered Emmett Till as Medgar pursued justice to bring the young boy's murderers to trial. Nothing could have shielded Medgar's eyes from the deplorable conditions of the Mississippi sharecroppers or from the "strange fruit" hung on trees by brutal barbarians.

When the struggle for freedom began in the late 1950s, the individuals participating in the civil rights movement could not possibly have foreseen that protesting in support of basic human dignity would culminate in one of the most heartrending civil wars of American history. The stories and the photographs seen in this book testify to the shameful conditions endured by black Americans during a period when democracy was being promoted and fought for on the international front. Most blacks in America lived without even the limited liberties afforded citizens of third-world countries. The faces that stare at you from the pages that follow are marked with the determination of individuals who were prepared to die for their own right to be free.

While some of the faces in these photographs reflect the scars and weary tears of battle fatigue, there are also visions of hope mirrored in the eyes of the warriors. A picture of the Little Rock Nine studying in quiet determination pending their admittance into the town's previously segregated high school offers evidence that we were moving in the right direction. Just three years before, the victorious 1954 decision of *Brown v. Board of Education* had struck down segregation in the nation's public schools, and it has also been applied to promoting equality in all aspects of American society. And who can forget the moving, spirited challenge of Fannie Lou Hamer's emotional testimony, when she moved the hearts of all those who heard her during the 1964 Democratic Convention. These are but two of the proud images to be seen in this work.

Every battle has its public and its private moments of defeat and victory. Every historical moment is made up of a multitude of personal experiences. Those battles and those experiences within the civil rights movement have been prolifically documented in written histories, but the camera has captured them with even greater force. For those of us who lived through these events, nothing brings them to mind more vividly than the extremely moving photographs seen here. They also serve to educate generations who were not alive during this provocative stage in our history. A young woman recently commented to me that she "hears so many speak about that period of time. It helps to hear the story, but we want—and need—more. Photos help because we can touch them and try to feel what it was like to live during that time."

As we search for answers to help us solve the pressing issues in this country, books such as this one will play a major part. Not only does it take us back to a period when events originated that would shape the American scene for years to come, but it also reinforces the need to address civil rights issues into the twenty-first century.

I find it difficult to look at these photographs without flinching from the memories and from the anger they invoke. But I must look. I must remember, as you must. For this was history in the making. Like it or not, you cannot hide from the camera's eye.

"Imprisoned in a Luminous Glare"

The civil rights movement cannot be understood without contemplating the photographs and the newsreel footage that presented it to an enormous audience. The persuasive and protective power of those pictures was recognized immediately. In *Why We Can't Wait,* his book on the Birmingham movement of 1963, the Reverend Martin Luther King, Jr., wrote about the media coverage of a campaign he had helped orchestrate: "The brutality with which officials would have quelled the black individual became impotent when it could not be pursued with stealth and remain unobserved. It was caught—as a fugitive from a penitentiary is often caught—in gigantic circling spotlights. It was imprisoned in a luminous glare revealing the naked truth to the whole world."[1]

King had in mind the already famous photographs of the Birmingham struggles—images of protesters attacked by police dogs and battered by high-pressure water cannons. His metaphor is apt: the media as a spotlight that exposes and thereby halts secret actions, a light that imprisons the imprisoners. King knew that cameras were helping to dismantle arsenals of oppression. The organizers of the Birmingham movement staged conflicts for the media to publicize. Some of the clashes between protesters and police became spectacles with immense visual resonance. The Birmingham photographs, published on front pages here and abroad, captured ruthless repression in extraordinarily vivid images. Scenes unthinkable to Americans as American were shown to America and all the world. Public sympathy and financial support, as well as political backing, flowed to movement organizations.

Because it was an essential Cold War strategy of the United States to project an image of Americans guarding and encouraging democracy around the world, the

SEGREGATED WATER FOUNTAINS, NORTH CAROLINA, 1950. **ELLIOTT ERWITT**

Birmingham photographs were an international embarrassment. President John F. Kennedy said that the Birmingham pictures on the front page of the *Washington Post* made him sick. Some of his queasiness no doubt resulted from having to explain those pictures to African leaders. As his aide Harris Wofford had written to him in 1962, on returning from an African tour, "Ending discrimination in America would do more to promote good relations with Africa than anything else."[2] It was partly in response to the Birmingham protests that Kennedy initiated the bill that, after his death, would become the Civil Rights Act of 1964.

The photographs of the civil rights movement constitute the deepest and broadest photographic documentation of any social struggle in America. Their quantity, variety, and quality found a new receptiveness on the part of white Americans to look at African-American struggles for liberation—struggles that dated back to emancipation and beyond that to slavery. This new openness was stimulated by new social factors and new ideologies, including postwar prosperity and Cold War antifascism. During the civil rights era, images of black struggles for equality entered many white homes for the first time.

SEE PAGE 21

In the past the white news media had ignored positive images of African-American life and suppressed portrayals of black political action. A clear example is cited by historian Nicholas Natanson. In New Madrid County, Missouri, during the winter of 1938–39, landowners sought to evict hundreds of black and white tenant farmers so that cheaper day laborers could be hired instead. Owen Whitfield, a black Baptist preacher and organizer for the Southern Tenant Farmers Union, persuaded the sharecroppers to mount a protest. Thirteen hundred of the displaced farmers pitched camp along a hundred-mile stretch of Highways 60 and 61. The protest received extensive coverage in newspapers across the nation, but blacks were given scant notice in the published reports and photographs, even though more than 90 percent of the protesters were black. The role of the black organizers was omitted altogether. Photographs that give a better indication of black activism were made by Arthur Rothstein (a Farm Security Administration photographer), but they were not published at the time.[3]

The Emmett Till lynching, in 1955, received a different kind of press coverage, extensive coverage that was new in America. Racial lynching—the abduction and murder of black men by white mobs—was the most extreme form of the physical intimidation that undergirded so much American racism prior to the civil rights movement. Lynching, a homegrown form of American terrorism used to scare off blacks from voting and seeking other rights, had begun in the Reconstruction era directly after the Civil War and was spread by the Ku Klux Klan. Walter Chivers, Martin Luther King, Jr.'s sociology professor at Morehouse College, estimated that in the South between 1880 and 1922 a lynching was perpetrated every two and a half days.[4] The law and the press ignored these murders even though they were often carried out in public, with advance notice and with the cooperation of leading white citizens.

Emmett Till was a fourteen-year-old black schoolboy visiting relatives near the hamlet called Money in the Mississippi Delta. Because he had prankishly flirted with a white shopkeeper, he was brutally beaten and shot. Several days later his corpse was found in the Tallahatchie River, with a gin-mill fan barbwired around his neck. The boy's mother, Mamie Bradley, insisted that his body be shipped back home to Chicago, where it was displayed in an open coffin for four days. At least a hundred thousand members of the black community stood in line for hours to view the body. The leading black periodicals, including *Jet* and the *Chicago Defender*, juxtaposed earlier photographs of the bright-eyed youngster in shirt and tie with the horrific picture of his bashed and bloated face. The story of the huge outpouring of sympathy—and the lynching behind it—was picked up by the white press as well.

The trial of Till's murderers resulted in acquittal (they later gave a full confession to writer William Bradford Huie for four thousand dollars). Black congressman Charles Diggs of Detroit, who attended the trial in Sumner, Mississippi, later commented that "the picture in *Jet* magazine showing Emmet Till's mutilation was probably the greatest media product in the last forty or fifty years, because that picture stimulated a lot of interest and anger on the part of blacks all over the country."[5]

Pictures and stories about Emmett Till's murder transformed many who would fight in the civil rights movement over the next decade. Joyce Ladner of Waynesboro, Mississippi, recalled: "As the search for the body went on, my older sister and I . . . wanted to be the first in line to buy the *Hattiesburg American*. Each day we pored over the clippings of the lynching we kept in our scrapbook, and cried: Emmett Till was about our age. . . . When we saw his bloated body in *Jet* magazine, we asked each other 'How could they do that to him? He's only a young boy.'"[6] Joyce and Dorrie Ladner would later become leading members of the Student Nonviolent Coordinating Committee (SNCC, pronounced "snick"). Anne Moody recalled, "Before Emmett Till's murder, I had known the fear of hunger, hell, and the Devil. But now there was a new fear known to me—the fear of being killed just because I was black. This was the worst of my fears. . . . I didn't know what one had to do or not to do as a Negro not to be killed." Moody was fifteen in 1955 and soon became active in the Congress of Racial Equality (CORE) and SNCC.[7]

Martin Luther King, Jr., and Rosa Parks would both acknowledge the impact of the Till case, which received considerable coverage in their local newspaper, the *Montgomery Advertiser*.[8] Just three months after the Till murder trial, Parks was arrested for protesting bus segregation laws, and the modern civil rights movement began its activist phase.

A studio portrait of a young man, a corpse recorded for a black newspaper, shots of political protests taken for major news agencies: the consequential images of the civil rights movement were made by many types of photographer—photojournalists, movement photographers, antimovement photographers, artists, and amateurs. Each had distinct commitments and points of view.

Most civil rights photographs were taken by professional photojournalists, who set out to record newsworthy events according to the professional principle of objectivity. Many of the pictures that turned out to be most important to the movement—pictures that inspired substantive support—were made by photojournalists who were hardly pro-movement and appeared in publications that were hardly liberal. The *Montgomery Advertiser,* where Charles Moore was chief photographer in the early 1960s, was a typically segregationist southern newspaper that relegated "Negro News" to a separate section. But Moore remembers: "The newspaper tried very hard to portray everything fairly. It could have ignored the civil rights story; a very conservative paper would have said, 'We're giving this troublemaker King too much publicity. Let's ignore him. Maybe it will die down.' Well, the Montgomery paper didn't do that."[9]

SEE PAGE 105

Some photojournalists covering the movement realized that they were recording crucial moments of a nation in transition, and they were inspired by that prescience of historical significance. Some, even in the South, were angered by the scenes of racist injustice that they witnessed and came to support the cause of civil rights, insinuating that support into their pictures.

African-American photographers made a significant contribution to civil rights photography. Whether working for the black press, for a movement organization, or (in a very few instances) for the white press, black photographers often had access to situations that white photographers did not. Their pictures almost always convey the sense that they were photographing their own leaders, their own enemies, their own fellow victims. Black photographers of the movement included Gordon Parks and Frank Dandridge working for *Life;* Robert Sengstacke of the *Chicago Defender;* Joffre Clark, Fred de Van, Bob Fletcher, Rufus Hinton, Julius Lester, Francis Mitchell, and Clifford Vaughs of SNCC; and freelancers Ernest Withers, Beuford Smith, and Robert Houston. (In addition, Johnson Publishing Co., the owners of *Jet* and *Ebony* magazines, employed a large staff of black photographers—most notably, Moneta Sleet, Jr. Unfortunately, their work is almost totally unavailable for exhibition or publication due to very strict control of permissions by Johnson Publishing.)

The civil rights movement in the United States flourished in the age of television. In 1953, 45 percent of American households had television; just three years later the number had jumped to over 83 percent. The Telstar I communications satellite began to enable worldwide television linkups in 1962; the March on Washington of 1963, the largest political demonstration in the United States to date, was one of the first events to be broadcast live around the world. Howard Zinn, a historian active in the movement, contrasted the "new abolitionists with the original abolitionists of a hundred years earlier": "The present movement . . . consists mostly of Negroes who make their pleas to the nation more by physical acts of sacrifice than by verbal declamation. Their task is made easier by modern mass communication, for the nation, indeed the whole world, can see them on the television screen or in newspaper photos—marching, praying, singing, demonstrating their message."[10]

Martin Luther King, Jr., made particularly "hot copy." His charismatic leadership style was photogenic and telegenic. King was indeed the most significant leader of a movement that had many leaders, but his primacy was often exaggerated. It was media shorthand to refer to King as *the* leader, to the movement as "King's movement." His attractiveness to the news media began with his first leadership role, in the Montgomery bus boycott of 1955, and peaked with his winning the Nobel Peace Prize in 1964 and with the successful 1965 campaign in Selma.

SEE PAGE 26

The movement took advantage of the media's greediness for that most valuable of photographic commodities—the image of extreme violence. The violence that engulfed the movement was sometimes warlike, and for the illustrated press these battles filled a gap between the Korean and Vietnamese Wars. Many civil rights photographs were given prominence in *Life* magazine. In the 1950s and '60s the weekly issue of *Life* was the single most important media organ, seen by more than half the adult population of the United States and reaching more people than any television program. *Life* preferred to present the movement through the iconography of war: uniformed forces, commanders and foot soldiers, armed attacks, the wounded, state funerals, and so on.

Often the images were of booted and helmeted state-employed thugs attacking civilians—an iconography of fascism that shocked many viewers into sympathy for the oppressed. Even more than those from Birmingham, the Selma, Alabama, images of 1965 had this effect. On March 7, 1965, ABC interrupted its prime-time broadcast of the film *Judgment at Nuremberg* with footage from Selma of state troopers stampeding and beating peaceful marchers. "The hideous parallel between Auschwitz and Selma was obvious, even to the insensitive," wrote Warren Hinkle and David Welsh in *Ramparts*. "The pictures from Selma were unpleasant; the juxtaposition of the Nazi Storm Troopers and the Alabama State Troopers made them unbearable."[11]

SEE PAGE 178

David Garrow's *Protest at Selma* carefully examines the reactions of the media, the public, and the politicians to the movement's protest strategies. Garrow concludes:

> Violence by segregationists, combined with what was generally portrayed and perceived as the movement's generally nonviolent nature and its highly legitimate goals, had the effect both of making the movement appear "extremely virtuous" in comparison to its opponents and of depicting racial segregation as far more brutal than the majority of white Americans previously realized. Needless to say, a very major role in creating those all-important perceptions and reactions among both the society at large and political actors in Washington was played by the media, particularly certain segments of it.[12]

If the movement was a war, then it was a war in which the propaganda offices on both sides played important roles. Both the civil rights organizations and the southern whites who opposed them so vigorously staged media events. Each side kept up a barrage of words and images meant to discomfit their enemies and promote themselves.

The enemies of the movement recognized how the media was being used against them. An Alabama congressman wrote about King: "He went to Selma with the set purpose of breaking the law so that he would be arrested. His love of publicity is above the sacredness of the laws of our land."[13] Southern officials were not long in instituting countermeasures. Sheriff Jim Clark of Selma, for example, had one of his deputies photograph protesters and distribute those photos to their employers, which often resulted in the protesters' being fired. Clark was also famous for setting up obstructions specifically to thwart photographers, for threatening and beating photographers, and for other tactics designed to dim the "luminous glare." In a famous bit of film footage, Clark's patience is being tried by a harangue from movement leader Rev. C. T. Vivian. While Vivian is explaining to Clark why the sheriff is like a Nazi, Clark shouts at a film crew, "Turn off those lights, they're shining in my eyes." They turn them off, then on again. Clark's deputy reaches toward the lens and pushes the cameraman back; immediately thereafter the camera records, shakily, Clark or his deputy punching Vivian in the jaw.

Danny Lyon, a photographer working for SNCC, recorded in his journal a conversation he had with some state troopers in Gadsden, Alabama, on June 27, 1963:

SEE PAGE 145

> I introduced myself as a photographer working for a quasi-fascist news agency in Chicago, and spent the next few hours in quasi-fascist conversation with the police. . . . (We spoke of mutual friends) You know Forman? [SNCC executive secretary James Forman] Is he up in Danville [Virginia]? . . . (I noticed an officer, sitting behind the wheel of his car was going through a pile of 8 × 10 photos). . . . (He said a *Birmingham News* man was sending him shots. Maybe I could send shots of Danville leaders to check against those in Gadsden?)

This conversation documents how police would use civil rights photographs to identify their enemies. It also demonstrates the kind of ruses used by photographers on both sides to get access and information. Some photographers did indeed function as double agents, working for opposing sides simultaneously.

Both Mississippi and Alabama set up "Sovereignty Commissions"—state agencies empowered to investigate "race mixing" and other real or imagined violations of state segregation laws. The bigger and more famous Mississippi Sovereignty Commission files are currently kept closed (a fight to open them is being waged), but the Alabama Sovereignty Commission files in the state archive in Montgomery are available to scholars. They contain a set of photographs that show how images were crafted to show the movement in a bad light. Pictures were taken at the end of the Selma to Montgomery march in 1965 by photographers in the employ of the Alabama Department of Public Safety (the state troopers). These included surveillance photographs as well as pictures connected to one of the main projects of the commission—an antimovement propaganda film that was, in fact, produced and distributed in the mid-sixties. These photographers set out to get "dirt" on the movement, and often they did that in the most literal way: pictures of dirty feet and overflowing trash receptacles. They also focused on what they considered another kind of "dirt"—physical contact between whites and blacks.

Movement organizations were much more creative in their approaches to photography and publicity. SNCC was the most energetic center of media outreach. SNCC's executive director, James Forman, is credited with being the group's publicity genius. In the spring of 1962 he hired Julian Bond, then a Morehouse College student and poet active in the Atlanta sit-ins, to become SNCC's director of communications. The SNCC Communications office, located in the Atlanta headquarters, became a crucial and wide-ranging operation. Bond immediately inaugurated the photographically illustrated *Student Voice*, SNCC's newsletter. One example of its efficacy: John Lewis (the future chairman of SNCC) saw in an early issue a Congress of Racial Equality advertisement for the first Freedom Ride and signed himself up.[14]

Bond spoke about the publicity and the fund-raising power of photographs:

> Remember a famous photograph—it was in *Life* magazine and then the *New York Times*—taken at the Selma March. . . . They've hit John [Lewis, who was leading the march] on the head and he's going down. That picture appeared in the *New York Times* the day after the beating occurred in a full page [fund-raising] ad for SCLC [the Southern Christian Leadership Conference], and that just burned us up [in SNCC]. If we had had the ability to do it, the technical ability to quickly have a picture taken, fly it to New York, get it in the *Times*, have the [advertising] copy all ready, or if we'd even thought in that way, we would have done it ourselves. . . . Our anger was directed at the [SCLC] bureaucrats who were there who were sucking money and our publicity, 'cause publicity was money. If you got your name in the *New York Times*, your organizational name in the *New York Times*, you could reprint that, send it out to your mailing list and they'd send you some dough.[15]

SEE PAGE 179

Besides fund-raising, another important task of the SNCC Communications office was to pressure reporters into covering stories they would otherwise ignore. Mary King, who became second in command of the office, has written about her "hot list" of relatively sympathetic reporters and how hard she worked contacting them. "I spent my days and nights telephoning our field offices or receiving incoming phone calls, and then telephoning the news media to place the stories obtained from our field secretaries. It was normal for me to work seven days a week and from twelve to sixteen hours a day."[16] King also wrote about another role played by the media:

With the exception of those involved at the time, no one knows how important the effective use of the news media was to our safety, and even our lives.

Whenever a field secretary was jailed or a church mass-meeting bombed, whenever night riders struck or firebombings occurred, whenever a local leader's home was shot into, or any other serious act perpetrated, Julian Bond and I went into high gear. The presence of a reporter at a jail or a telephone inquiry from a newspaper was often the only step that let a local sheriff know he was being watched. Our job, in mobilizing the press, was to make local law officers feel that they were under scrutiny, thereby providing a measure of safety for civil rights workers.[17]

Movement organizations courted press photographers and staged media events. But the pictures made by outside photographers were not sufficient—too sparse and too superficial—so movement photography was fostered. As Mary King put it in a 1964 SNCC conference paper: "It is no accident that SNCC workers have learned that if our story is to be told, we will have to write it and photograph it and disseminate it ourselves." This important strategy has been largely ignored; it is never mentioned in any history of photography or of activist or political art.

Movement-originated photographs were both artistic expressions and instruments for organizing. Like the justly famous freedom songs of the movement, they were aids to understanding feelings and strategies, to cementing solidarity, and to spreading the passion. Movement photographs were circulated within the ranks, hung on walls of "freedom houses" and offices, disseminated as posters and in movement publications. Many civil rights leaders took photographs themselves as an adjunct to their work, including James Forman and Robert Zellner of SNCC, Rev. Wyatt T. Walker and Andrew Young of the SCLC, and Malcolm X. Several progressive groups expressly supported movement photographers, including the SCLC, the National Council of Churches, the Congress of Racial Equality, the Taconic Foundation, and the Highlander Folk School.

SNCC was the prime mover, under the initiative and guidance of James Forman. Not only did Forman recognize the ability of photographs to bear witness as events unfolded, he also spoke about the need to transcribe events for the historical record. Starting with Forman's recruitment of Danny Lyon in 1962, SNCC enlisted and helped train about a dozen photographers. There was a SNCC darkroom in Atlanta and another in Tougaloo, Mississippi. SNCC set up several networks for distributing its pictures and helped support the Southern Documentary Project, which sought to record the cultural and geographic contexts of the movement as well as its dramatic events. SNCC published photographic pamphlets and posters. It organized the first book of civil rights photography *(The Movement)* and an early exhibition *(US,* presented in 1967 at the Countee Cullen Library in Harlem).

In 1971 the writer Pat Watters asked John Lewis about mainstream media coverage

SEE PAGE 201

of the movement. He replied: "Any time there was some violence, we would get a story on television. But when we were involved in in-depth experiences, when people gathered to express feeling, spirit, like in the nonviolent workshops, there was no press. There was seldom an in-depth story on things like when white people really did change."[18]

Movement photography tried to correct this skewed vision of the mainstream press. Danny Lyon's photographs for SNCC succeeded in capturing both the day-to-day grind and the charged spirit of the movement. Lyon was not working on a newsman's deadline. He had time to hang around with people he loved and respected, photographing quiet moments and hot ones. For a while he shared an apartment in Atlanta with SNCC activist John Lewis and Sam Shirah. Lyon has written, "That a black and a white from Alabama and a New York Jew were all close friends and actually lived together says something very important about the cross fertilizations that were going on throughout the movement."[19] Lyon had a photographic vision that went to the heart of his subject without neglecting subsidiary details that convey the specifics of place, era, and personality.

The great photographs of the civil rights movement were crafted with urgent passion—for their own time and for the future. Reappearing now in books and exhibitions, in movies and electronic networks, they make us ask what it is to be white or black in America, to be powerful or powerless or empowered. No other American pictures radiate so brightly a collective passion for justice. These are photographs of participation, collaboration, struggle, and jubilation. The courageous participants in the movement rode and walked the highways together, sat down where they were not invited, danced in the parks and streets, sang on the stairs of power. They were forbidden to do these things, but they did them anyway. Fists and guns were thrust in their faces, clubs and fangs and water cannons punished their bodies, but they did not stop. These people stood up to power and took some of that power for themselves. But since power did not concede willingly, as it never does, many of these pictures are nightmare images of struggle and brutal repression and bereavement. There are pictures in this book that cry out at modern injustice with a disquieting appeal that rivals anything in the canons of modern art.

The black-led civil rights movement was the most momentous social struggle in postwar America. It was a "Second American Revolution" that forced America to reaffirm its democratic ideals and brought to light, as never before, the tunnels of injustice that have always undermined our democracy. The civil rights movement marched our democracy up to a new plateau. It was the model for the subsequent social movements of our era. Its vision and its methods continue to inspire and instruct struggles for justice around the world. "We Shall Overcome," the civil rights anthem, has been sung in recent years in Tiananmen Square, in Leipzig, in Johannesburg.

But the achievements of the civil rights movement fell far short of the racial equality that it envisioned. Racial hierarchies and hysterias continue to tear nation and neighborhood apart. In many ways, things have gotten worse in the United States since the civil rights era. The scandal of American inequality progresses shamelessly. In 1989, 1 percent of the population owned 37 percent of the wealth; 86 percent of the wealth was controlled by 10 percent of the people.[20] In 1992, 33.3 percent of black Americans had incomes below the poverty line, compared to 11.6 percent of whites.[21] African Americans continue to fare worse economically than any other racial group in the United States.

In 1981, in a new introduction to his novel *Invisible Man*, Ralph Ellison wrote: "So if the ideal of achieving a true political equality eludes us in reality—as it continues to do—there is still available that fictional vision of an ideal democracy in which the actual combines with the ideal and gives us representations of a state of things in which the highly placed and the lowly, the black and the white, the Northerner and the Southerner, and the native-born and the immigrant are combined to tell us of transcendent truths and possibilities."[22] Such truths and possibilities infuse these photographs of the civil rights movement. They are an essential part of our vision of a true democracy. They are documents that can inspire us to find new ways out of our current morass. We must look at these pictures and feel embarrassment and fear and rage. We must look at them and feel hope. We must look at them to learn new ways to transform our nation.

"BLACK CHILDREN AND WHITE DOLL," 1942.
GORDON PARKS

In the 1940s black psychologist Kenneth Clark studied the internalization of racist stereotypes by interviewing children about the color of the dolls they preferred. His findings—that many black children had been taught to consider themselves inferior—played a crucial role in convincing the U.S. Supreme Court in 1954 that "separate, but equal" public schools were inherently discriminatory against black children.

Gordon Parks made this picture while working for the Farm Security Administration. He believed that "what the camera had to do was expose the evils of racism, the evils of poverty, the discrimination and the bigotry, by showing the people who suffered the most under it."

LYNCHING, MARION, INDIANA, AUGUST 9, 1930.
BEITLER STUDIO

"Two Negroes were taken from the Grand County jail at Marion, Ind. and hung to a tree in the public square after they had been accused on charges of murdering Claude Deeter, 23, and assaulting his girl friend, 19-year-old Mary Ball. Photo shows Abram Smith, 19 (left) and Thomas Shipp, 18 (right) hanging from the tree shortly after they had been strung up." (Original UPI caption.)

A third suspect, James Cameron, age sixteen, was also taken to the lynching; he watched his two friends being murdered, but escaped their fate. Cameron is the founder and director of the Black Holocaust Museum in Milwaukee.

EVICTION PROTEST OFF HIGHWAY 61, NEW MADRID, MISSOURI, JANUARY 10, 1939. **ASSOCIATED PRESS**

"Hundreds of sharecroppers—the Highway Patrol estimated 1,000 of them—marched with their belongings to U.S. No. 61 near here and encamped. They said eviction notices had been served on them. Highway patrol Sergeant R. R. Reed said most of them came here from other states, occupied any farm buildings available for temporary shelter while pick-ing cotton and now that the picking season is over, haven't funds with which to get home." (Original AP caption.)

This uninformative photograph and deceptive caption illustrate press hostility toward black protest before the civil rights era.

BELOW: EMMETT TILL IN HIS CASKET, RAYNER'S
FUNERAL PARLOR, CHICAGO, SEPTEMBER 1955.
CHICAGO DEFENDER

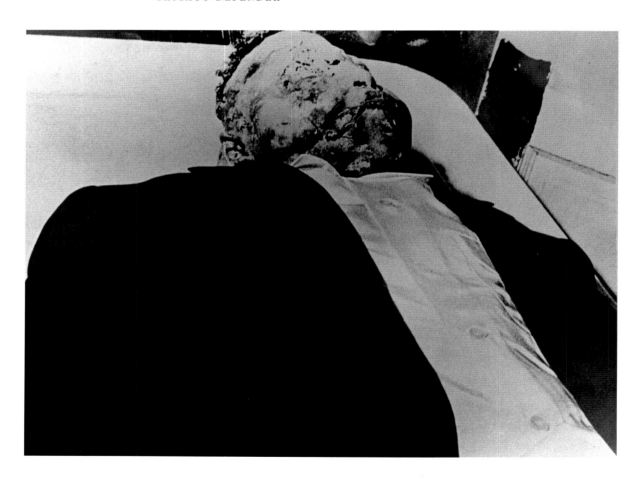

OPPOSITE: MOSES "PREACHER" WRIGHT—ON THE WITNESS
STAND IN SUMNER, MISSISSIPPI, SEPTEMBER 22, 1955—
POINTS TO THE MEN ACCUSED OF MURDERING HIS GRAND-
NEPHEW EMMETT TILL. **JOE MIGON**

When J. W. Milam and Ray Bryant kidnapped Emmett Till from his granduncle's house, they told the sixty-four-year-old sharecropper, "Preacher, if you cause any trouble you'll never live to be sixty-five." Wright's bravery in accusing the two white men of murder in a southern court was unprecedented. He pointed first to Milam, saying "Thar he," then pointed out Bryant. He sat down, according to *New York Post* reporter Murray Kempton, "with a lurch which told better than any-thing else the cost in strength to him of the thing he had done." Wright remembered feeling "the blood boil in hundreds of white people as they sat glaring in the courtroom. It was the first time in my life that I had the courage to accuse a white man of a crime, let alone something terrible as killing a boy. I wan't exactly brave and I wasn't scared. I just wanted to see justice done." Unable to remain safely in Mississippi after testifying, Wright moved to Chicago.

"EMERGING MAN," HARLEM, 1952. **GORDON PARKS**

In 1952 Ralph Ellison published *Invisible Man*, his great novel of a search for African-American identity. The "invisible man" begins his story speaking from his basement "hole" residence. "I am invisible, understand, simply because people refuse to see me. Like the bodiless heads you see sometimes in circus sideshows, it is as though I have been surrounded by mirrors of hard, distorting glass. When they approach me they see only my surroundings, themselves, or figments of their imagination—indeed, everything and anything except me."

This is one of several illustrations that Parks made for a story about *Invisible Man*. Ellison and Parks were good friends; parts of *Invisible Man* were written in Parks's home.

A REPORTER, RALPH ABERNATHY, DAN WEINER,
AND KING SHARE A JOKE, MONTGOMERY, 1956.
UNKNOWN PHOTOGRAPHER

Dan Weiner, on assignment from *Collier's* magazine, was the first photographer to capture the importance of the Montgomery movement and its young leader, Martin Luther King, Jr. Weiner wrote:

> It was a question of the whole community suddenly rearing up on its hind legs and challenging the powers that be. There was a new Black in the South who was developing a new strategy of resistance to segregation with economic, legal, and spiritual weapons. I felt that photography had to look at the whole social scene more

broadly and to go into it more deeply. My point was to show the great forces struggling here in one area. I felt that this was an historic occasion that I must try to record with my camera.

> While I was in Montgomery, I thought of something that Alan Paton had said to me in 1954 when we traveled together on a story on the Negro in America. He said, "These people, through their struggles to achieve their basic rights as citizens, are reeducating us as to the meaning of true Americanism."

LEFT: REFUSE AT THE MONTGOMERY AIRPORT AFTER THE SELMA TO MONTGOMERY MARCH, MARCH 25, 1965. **ALABAMA DEPARTMENT OF PUBLIC SAFETY**

BELOW: FOLKSINGER JOAN BAEZ (LEFT) WITH UNIDENTIFIED MARCHER AT THE RALLY AT THE END OF THE SELMA TO MONTGOMERY MARCH, MARCH 25, 1965. **ALABAMA DEPARTMENT OF PUBLIC SAFETY**

LEFT: KU KLUX KLAN RALLY, NEAR SALISBURY, NORTH CAROLINA, 1964 OR 1965. **CHARLES MOORE**

Pictured here is the Grand Dragon of North Carolina, James R. (Bob) Jones, accompanied by two unidentified Klanswomen.

Founded in 1866, the Ku Klux Klan was the most notorious white terror organization in the United States. Klansmen donned their white shrouds to masquerade as Rebel soldiers risen from hell. Their founding purpose was to keep blacks from voting. Rising and falling in power over the years, with six million members at its height, the Klan has played a significant role in U.S. politics. Klansmen committed many of the murders and other crimes of the civil rights era.

In the spring of 1951 W. Eugene Smith was in South Carolina working on a photo-essay about Maude Callen, a dedicated black midwife. One Saturday night he sought out a Klan meeting "and photographed by the light of the flaming cross."

Smith wrote to his mother about the trip:

> I admit the KKK meeting was a strong dose of poison to receive at the beginning. The leaders spoke in warped vicious hatred that disregarded truth almost completely, while the majority of the "common folk" who agreed spoke out of ignorance warped by the ravings of the leaders. . . . The majority are not necessarily right. They are told and they repeat, and it is because of this the obligation of my profession lays so heavily upon my conscience to weigh and balance all that I photograph and all that I ultimately state in public.

OPPOSITE: "WILLIAM CASBY, BORN IN SLAVERY, ALGIERS, LOUISIANA, MARCH 24, 1963." **RICHARD AVEDON**

Avedon made this portrait while traveling in the South for his book *Nothing Personal.* He and the writer James Baldwin had been classmates at De Witt Clinton High School in the Bronx, where they coedited the school literary magazine. In 1963 they collaborated on *Nothing Personal.* A study of the faces of power and powerlessness in America, it includes numerous pictures of civil rights workers and their opponents.

1.

"My Soul Is Rested"

"Y'all make it light on yourself and let me have those seats," shouted driver J. P. Blake at four black passengers on his bus. They hadn't jumped up fast enough when a white rider stood over them, demanding that they move to the back of the bus. Three of the four did change seats. But Rosa Parks, a forty-three-year-old seamstress on her way home from work, refused. Blake told her he would enforce Montgomery's segregation laws and have her arrested. Parks replied quietly, "You may do that."[1]

Parks was taken to jail, booked, fingerprinted, photographed, and locked in a cell. Allowed one call, she phoned home. Her mother answered and could not help asking, "Did they beat you?"[2] Parks reassured her mother, who then phoned E. D. Nixon, the person in Montgomery that blacks were most likely to call when they were in civil rights trouble. Nixon was an officer of the Brotherhood of Sleeping Car Porters, the black union founded by A. Philip Randolph. Nixon had headed the local branch of the March on Washington Movement in 1941, which had pressured President Franklin D. Roosevelt to integrate the defense industries during World War II. In 1943, when he was state president of the National Association for the Advancement of Colored People (NAACP), Nixon helped Parks become secretary of Montgomery's NAACP, a post she had held ever since.

Parks also founded and advised the local NAACP Youth Council. Over the years she and her charges had made defiant attempts to integrate Montgomery's libraries and buses. Nixon said, "If there ever was a woman devoted to the cause, Rosa Parks was that woman."[3]

Nixon, too, feared for Parks's safety in jail. He arrived promptly, accompanied by lawyer Clifford Durr and Durr's wife, Virginia—Montgomery's prominent white integrationists. Longtime admirers of Parks's political commitment, the Durrs had helped to arrange her recent participation in interracial workshops at the Highlander Folk School

in Monteagle, Tennessee—the South's leading integrationist study center. Nixon and the Durrs found out that Parks had been charged with violating the Alabama bus segregation laws. They posted bond for Mrs. Parks and took her home.

During the rejoicing at this escape from immediate danger, Nixon and Clifford Durr conferred out of earshot. They realized that this might be the desired case, the case to challenge in court the abuses that blacks faced daily on the Montgomery bus system. Several recent arrests had stirred indignation and discussions of action, but each of those cases had been flawed in some way. Parks was the ideal person to unite Montgomery's fractured black community. She was tirelessly devoted to both church and civil rights activities, she was respected by all who met her. She combined a working-class background with a dignified demeanor that would impress even white judges. Nixon asked Parks if she was willing to fight the charges. In terror, her husband interjected, "The white folks will kill you, Rosa." After some thought, Parks offered, "If you think it will mean something to Montgomery and do some good, I'll be happy to go along with it."[4]

Jo Ann Robinson, an Alabama State College professor of English who headed the Woman's Political Caucus (WPC), was ready to act when she heard of the Parks arrest. The caucus had been formed in 1949 to encourage black women to register to vote. It was also active in fighting bus-system abuses, such as the recent arrest of Claudette Colvin—a case that Parks had worked on as well. There had been talk of a court challenge, even of a bus boycott, until it was discovered that Miss Colvin was pregnant. There was no impediment with Parks. Robinson called the other WPC leaders, and they decided to implement their plan for a one-day bus boycott. Montgomery's civil rights community was mobilizing around one of its most respected members.

Rosa Parks was arrested on Thursday evening, December 1, 1955. By Friday morning, Robinson, along with her colleagues and students, had commandeered a college mimeograph machine, run off a mountain of thirty-five thousand handbills, and begun to distribute them throughout the city. (The WPC had chosen leafleting as the means of communication because Montgomery's fifty thousand African Americans had no radio station and no widely read newspaper.) The third paragraph of the leaflet read: "The woman's case will come up on Monday. We are therefore asking every Negro to stay off the buses Monday in protest of the arrest and trial. Don't ride the buses to work, to town, to school, or anywhere on Monday."[5] Over the weekend the leaflets reached the majority of Montgomery's blacks. Others were alerted by a front-page story in Sunday's *Montgomery Advertiser*, the leading white paper. Nixon had contacted a friendly local reporter, promising him "the hottest story you've ever written."[6]

SEE PAGE 41

PREVIOUS PAGE: MARTIN LUTHER KING, JR., AND RALPH ABERNATHY ON THE FIRST DESEGREGATED BUS, MONTGOMERY, DECEMBER 21, 1956. **ERNEST WITHERS**
On the far left is Glenn Smiley of the Fellowship of Reconciliation, an influential pacifist organization founded in England in 1914.

At five o'clock Friday morning, after conferring with Robinson, Nixon had started phoning Montgomery's black ministers and other leaders. He wanted to reach "the people who represent peoples."[7] The first and second calls were to the progressive ministers Ralph Abernathy and H. H. Hubbard. They immediately agreed to support the boycott and to attend an organizational meeting that evening. Third called was the recently appointed twenty-six-year-old minister of the Dexter Avenue Baptist Church, Rev. Martin Luther King, Jr. King asked if he could think about it awhile. When Nixon called him back later, he became the nineteenth leader to give his support. "I'm glad you agreed," Nixon told King, "because I already set the meeting up to meet at your church."[8]

Dexter Avenue Baptist was a small but influential church known for the relative prosperity of its three hundred members and the erudition of its ministers. It had a prime location at the end of Montgomery's main street; only the white stone headquarters of the state police stood between it and the monumental state capitol. The capitol had earned Montgomery the title "Cradle of the Confederacy" because it was there in 1861 that Jefferson Davis took his oath as first president of the Confederate States of America. Nixon knew that Dexter's central location would encourage a large turnout for Friday's crucial strategy meeting.

In fact, the turnout was impressive, bringing together over forty leaders of Montgomery's black communities. They backed the boycott unanimously and then broke up into committees to work out the logistics for Monday: emergency transport, additional publicity, and all the other practicalities.

Jo Ann Robinson described the day of the boycott:

> At 5:30 Monday, December 5, dawn was breaking over Montgomery. Early morning workers were congregating at corners. There, according to plan, Negroes were to be picked up not by the Montgomery City Lines, but by Negro taxis driving at reduced rates of ten cents per person, or by some two hundred private cars which had been offered free to bus riders for Monday only.
>
> The suspense was almost unbearable, for no one was positively sure that the taxi drivers would keep their promises, that the private car owners would give absolute strangers a ride, that Negro bus riders would stay off the bus. And then there was the cold and the threat of rain.[9]

Up early were Martin Luther King, Jr., and his wife, Coretta Scott King. He described their excitement in his first book, *Stride toward Freedom: The Montgomery Story.* "'Martin, Martin, come quickly!' I put down my cup and ran toward the living room. As I approached the front window Coretta pointed joyfully to a slowly moving bus: 'Darling, it's empty!'" King jumped in his car to check out the city at large, finding that "instead of the 60 per cent cooperation we had hoped for, it was becoming apparent that we had reached almost 100 per cent. A miracle had taken place. The once dormant and quiescent Negro community was now fully awake."[10]

King watched the boycotters. "During the rush hour the sidewalks were crowded with laborers and domestic workers, many of them well past middle age, trudging patiently to their jobs and home again, sometimes as much as twelve miles. They knew why they walked, and the knowledge was evident in the way they carried themselves. And as I watched them I knew that there is nothing more majestic than the determined courage of individuals willing to suffer and sacrifice for their freedom and dignity."[11]

Elsewhere that Monday morning Rosa Parks was convicted of violating segregation laws; she was fined ten dollars plus four dollars for court costs and given a suspended jail sentence. Black attorney Fred Gray filed an appeal. When Nixon went to arrange for Parks's release, he saw something at the courthouse he had never seen before. Instead of just a few timid relatives of the accused, in the halls and tumbling out onto the street was a crowd of some five hundred supporters. Nixon was alarmed by the boldness of this new kind of demonstration and by the shotguns that the policemen now had in their hands.

A group gathered at three o'clock to plan the mass meeting scheduled for that evening at Holt Street Baptist Church. They agreed to form an ad hoc organization and started discussing its leadership. One faction wanted to hide the identities of the leaders, but Nixon, a seasoned organizer, responded furiously: "What the hell you people talkin' about? How you gonna have a mass meeting, gonna boycott a city bus line without the white folks knowing about it? You guys went around here and lived off these poor washwomen all your lives and ain't never done nothing for 'em. . . . You oughta make up your mind right now that you gon' either admit you are a grown man or concede the fact that you are a bunch of scared boys."[12]

Nixon's reproach was answered by a latecomer just walking into the meeting, Martin Luther King, Jr. "Mr. Nixon, I'm not a coward, I don't want anybody to call me a coward."[13] He agreed with Nixon that openness would be the best course. Next, Rufus Lewis—funeral director, football coach, voting rights advocate, and member of Dexter Avenue Baptist—jumped up to nominate King for president of the yet-unnamed organization. The young pastor may have been favored for having stood up to Nixon, or for his reputed integrity and gifted oratory, or because as a newcomer he still lacked enemies, or because others were reluctant to take the dangerous helm. For whatever reasons, no other nominations were forwarded, and King was elected head of the Montgomery Improvement Association (MIA). (The name was coined by King's closest friend, Rev. Ralph Abernathy.)

Should the boycott be continued? That would be decided at the mass meeting in less than an hour. The new MIA president rushed home to prepare the keynote speech and to tell his wife the news. Though mindful of the dangers that her husband's new position could bring, she nevertheless offered her blessing and support. King would usually spend upward of fifteen hours writing a Sunday sermon; now he had just twenty minutes to prepare the first political address of his life. He was stricken by fear of this new responsibility. Suddenly his parish had ballooned to include the fifty thousand members of Montgomery's black community, and television cameras would project his speech even beyond the city. King prayed for guidance and managed to shake off his paralysis with only fifteen minutes left to outline the speech. Above all, he wanted to strike a balance between moderacy and militancy. King had been stung by comparisons being made between the boycotters and segregationist "protesters" like the Ku Klux Klan. He would stress the lawfulness of the black protest and its core of Christian love.

The Holt Street Baptist Church was jammed. This meeting would determine the fate of the boycott. Hundreds of boycotters were inside; loudspeakers were set up for the several thousand more who overflowed onto the street. "Onward Christian Soldiers" was sung, then King began to speak. He spoke about the bravery of Rosa Parks and the "height of her character." His phrases were punctuated with the listeners' shouts and applause. "You know my friends there comes a time when people get tired of being trampled over by the iron feet of oppression." Shouts and foot stomping came from inside and out of the church—louder than King had ever heard before at a religious or political rally. He concluded: "Let us go out with a grim and bold determination that we are going to stick together. . . . Right here in Montgomery when the history books are written in the future, somebody will have to say, 'There lived a race of people, black people, fleecy locks and black complexions, of people who had the moral courage to stand up for their rights, and thereby they injected a new meaning into the veins of history and of civilization."[14]

When the applause subsided, Abernathy rose to put forward the demands that the association had drafted. They did not call for the end of segregation on the buses, though that had already been achieved in several other southern cities. Their three demands were moderate: courteous treatment of all passengers, first-come-first-served segregated seating, and the hiring of some black drivers. The resolution was put that the boycott would continue until these demands were met. The voters inside and out passed the motion unanimously. Abernathy recalled, "The fear left that had shackled us across the years—all left suddenly when we were in that church together."[15]

Montgomery had become the cradle of the modern civil rights movement. The boycott would continue unbroken for more than twelve months—twelve months of deep cooperation among Montgomery's black citizens, a community that knit itself together with hardly a lost stitch. The strains of trudging to work and worrying about a dangerous and uncertain cause were eased by feelings of solidarity and righteousness. An elderly walker, Mother Pollard, said it most succinctly: "My feets is weary, but my soul is rested."

On the fourth day of the boycott, representatives of the MIA presented their three demands at a meeting with the city commissioners and bus company executives. They were refused. Bus company attorney Jack Crenshaw argued, "If we granted the Negro these demands, they would go about boasting of a victory they had won over the white people, and this we will not stand for." King was shocked by their intransigence. "I had believed that the privileged would give up their privileges upon request," he later wrote. "I came to see that no one gives up his privileges without strong resistance."[16]

SEE PAGE 44

The MIA started to prepare for a long haul. Police Commissioner Clyde Sellers had indicated that he would not tolerate the black-driven taxis charging fares below the regulated minimum, which ruled them out; a reliable car pool system would be essential. King called his college friend Rev. T. J. Jemison, who had led a successful two-week bus boycott in Baton Rouge, Louisiana, in the summer of 1953. With Jemison's experience and advice in mind, King explained to the evening's mass meeting the nature and necessity of a car pool. First, he assured the gathering that the MIA could handle the funding of the operations. Then he spoke of the hard sacrifices to come. King asked teachers and businessmen to chauffeur road crews and housemaids. He asked young men to open their shining new cars, the best things they ever hoped to own, to total strangers. Hesitantly, he volunteered the ministers first. The response to King's suggestions was tremendous. Over 150 stepped forward to pledge their cars. Normal proprieties were set aside as the entire black community drew close together.

Within days an efficient transport system was in operation. Forty-eight dispatch and forty-two pickup stations were established. Funding came from within the community and from without. Workers were said to be donating one out of five dollars of their weekly salaries. Collections were taken at the biweekly mass meetings. Contributions came from the NAACP, Montgomery's Jewish community, the United Auto Workers, anonymous white southerners, elementary school classes, a Swiss matron, and numerous other sources. The funds paid for gas, repairs, and countless other needs. Eventually, the MIA was able to purchase several station wagons of its own.

When the boycott didn't simply peter out as expected, white counterattacks began. The Men of Montgomery, an association of prominent white businessmen, alarmed by the loss of black customers, made overtures toward compromise. But the all-white city government, led by three commissioners, instituted a "get-tough" policy. By January 24 all three commissioners had joined the White Citizens Council, the "white-collar Klan," whose Montgomery branch went from six thousand to twelve thousand members over the next month. Police Commissioner Sellers volunteered to spearhead the boycott busting; he proclaimed at a council rally: "I don't have any Negro customers!"[17] Intensive police harassment of black drivers began: flurries of tickets were issued for speeding, for driving too slowly, for tiny infractions and for fabricated ones.

On Thursday, January 26, an officer pulled over Martin Luther King, Jr., and told him, "Get out, King; you are under arrest for speeding thirty miles an hour in a twenty-five mile zone."[18] When the squad car drove him over the river, out of town, King began to fear for his life. Then he saw the sign for the Montgomery City Jail and felt a twisted relief— and embarrassment that he hadn't realized where his comrades had been taken all those weeks. King was shut behind bars for the first time in his life. He was appalled by the smell of the open toilet. To his cell mates asking him for help he cracked: "Fellows, before I can assist in getting any of you out, I've got to get my ownself out."[19] Eventually, Abernathy ushered his friend out of jail through an anxious crowd of supporters.

Jo Ann Robinson had a brick thrown through her picture window and her car pitted with acid—by policemen. Numerous other acts of violence and sabotage were committed. The commissioners plotted to short-circuit the boycott by announcing to the press that they had reached a settlement with a delegation of "prominent Negro ministers." Fortuitously, the press release was noticed on the Associated Press wire by Carl Rowan, a black writer for the *Minneapolis Tribune* who had recently covered the Montgomery story. Rowan's telephone call to King led to exposure of the attempted hoax.

Such attacks only intensified the black demands, a pattern that would be repeated throughout the history of the civil rights movement. On Monday, January 30, the MIA executive board voted to file suit in U.S. District Court challenging the constitutionality of segregated buses. The struggle could no longer be limited to half-measures. King announced the bold decision to a mass meeting late that evening. Mother Pollard, who had the privileges of the veteran fighter, called King down to her from his lectern. "I knows something is wrong. Is it that we ain't doing things to please you? Or is it that the white folks is bothering you?" As King smiled, she moved closer. "I done told you we is with you all the way. But even if we ain't with you, God's gonna take care of you." King felt tears coming on and a kind of energized fearlessness.[20]

Minutes later Abernathy informed King that his house had been bombed; the condition of Coretta and their ten-week-old daughter, Yolanda, was not yet known. King took a moment to calm the church, then sped home. He pushed through a dangerously enraged crowd of several hundred supporters—some holding guns or knives. He found Coretta and "Yoki" unharmed. "Why don't you get dressed, darling?" Martin whispered to Coretta, who was still in her bathrobe.[21] Commissioner Sellers appeared and promised to catch the bombers. "Regrets are fine, Mr. Sellers, but you created the atmosphere for this bombing with your 'get tough' policy."[22] The speaker was C. T. Smiley, the principal of Booker T. Washington High School, whose words were especially brave since Sellers paid his salary.

As news cameras rolled, King calmed the crowd. "If you have weapons, take them home. 'He who lives by the sword will perish by the sword.' Remember that is what Jesus said. We are not advocating violence. We want to love our enemies. Be good to them. This is what we must live by. We must meet hate with love."[23]

Two days later Nixon's house was bombed. And there would be many more bombings during the boycott—of homes, churches, and car pool stations. These terrorist acts were committed by government officials and by members of racist militias like the Ku Klux Klan; often the terrorists were both.

On February 21, 1956, eighty-nine indictments were handed down under an almost forgotten law that forbade conspiracies to boycott "without just cause." King was the one and only defendant to be tried. His trial was covered by an international corps of journalists; his conviction made front pages across the nation. He was on the cover of *Jet,* he was profiled in the *New York Times;* his worldwide fame had begun.

SEE PAGE 46

The boycott continued through the spring, summer, and fall of 1956. Workers walked, car pools rolled, and the antisegregation case crawled through the federal courts. Meanwhile, the city filed a potentially devastating injunction against the MIA, seeking the cessation of carpooling and a large fine. King sat in court on November 13, extremely pessimistic. He was obliged to deny remembering how the boycott had been organized. At noon a reporter plunged into the courtroom and handed King an Associated Press bulletin announcing the U.S. Supreme Court's decision affirming the unconstitutionality of Alabama's bus-segregation laws. King dashed to the spectator seats to tell the news to Coretta, Abernathy, and Nixon. One bystander burst out: "God Almighty has spoken from Washington, D.C."[24]

That evening ecstatic mass meetings were held to celebrate the victory. But troubles continued. The Supreme Court decision unleashed deadly threats from white racists. One night the Ku Klux Klan rode in force through black neighborhoods. They were greeted not by dark and silent streets but by bright porch lights, Sunday clothes, waving handkerchiefs, and applause—a totally new response. The Klansmen drove off sheepishly. Such victories yielded both newfound courage and stepped-up bombings and shootings of black targets.

The black community—but not the white—actively prepared for a peaceful transition to desegregation. There were training sessions in techniques of nonviolence. Trainees acted out the roles of hostile driver, taunting racist rider, nonviolent rider, and so on. A mimeographed broadside called "Suggestions for Integrating Buses" was distributed. Its seventeen suggestions included: "If cursed, do not curse back. If pushed, do not push back. If struck, do not strike back, but evidence love and goodwill at all times." And, "For the first few days try to get on the bus with a friend in whose non-violence you have confidence. You can uphold one another by a glance or a prayer."[25]

At 5:45 on the morning of December 21, 1956, the first integrated bus rolled through Montgomery. As he climbed on board, King was greeted by the driver with a cordial "We are glad to have you this morning." King sat down on a front seat with Glenn Smiley, the white minister who had been an MIA adviser. Also on the first bus were Abernathy, Nixon, attorney Fred Gray, and a troop of photographers, cameramen, and reporters.

Years later Jo Ann Robinson still savored the victory of the Montgomery bus boycott:

We had won self-respect. We had won a feeling that we had achieved, had accomplished. We felt that we were somebody, that somebody had to listen to us, that we had forced the white man to give what we knew was a part of our citizenship. If you have never had the feeling that this is the other man's country and you are an alien in it, but that this is your country, too, then you don't know what I'm talking about. But it is a hilarious feeling that just goes all over you, that makes you feel that America is a great country and we're going to do more to make it greater.[26]

ROSA PARKS AT THE HIGHLANDER FOLK SCHOOL,
MONTEAGLE, TENNESSEE, JULY 1956. **IDA BERMAN**

The summer before her arrest on the Montgomery bus, Rosa Parks had spent her vacation at the Highlander Folk School. She returned to Highlander the following summer, in the midst of the boycott.

Ida Berman, a labor union photographer associated with the Photo League in New York, was visiting Highlander with a friend when its director, Myles Horton, asked her to make portraits of Parks and Septima Clark. Horton later invited Berman to photograph Highlander's Literacy and Citizenship Program on Johns Island, South Carolina.

SEPTIMA CLARK LEADING A CITIZENSHIP-EDUCATION
CLASS, JOHNS ISLAND, SOUTH CAROLINA, JANUARY 16–23,
1959. **IDA BERMAN**

On both occasions that Rosa Parks visited the Highlander Folk School, she attended workshops led by Septima Clark. A major grassroots organizer in the civil rights movement, Clark (seated center) had a legendary ability to prepare illiterate adults for voter-registration exams and then guide those same students into becoming teachers themselves. In 1956 she was recruited by founder-director Myles Horton to become Highlander's director of workshops. Her program was subsequently transferred to the SCLC, where she became supervisor of teacher training.

To Clark's left is Alice Wine, a citizenship student and founding member of the Progressive Club, a cooperative food store and community center. Standing behind is Bernice Robinson, a leading citizenship teacher; three other students are also shown.

ROSA PARKS BEING FINGERPRINTED, MONTGOMERY,
FEBRUARY 22, 1956. **ASSOCIATED PRESS**

"WOMAN FINGERPRINTED—Mrs. Rosa Parks, Negro
seamstress whose refusal to move to the back of the bus
touched off the bus boycott of Montgomery, Ala., last
December, is fingerprinted by Deputy Sheriff D. H. Lackey
in Montgomery, Feb. 22. Mrs. Parks, whose appeal on a
$14 fine for violating segregation laws was turned down, is
among the 100 or so Montgomery Negroes indicted by a
grand jury on anti-boycott charges." (Original AP caption.)

BOYCOTTED BUS, MONTGOMERY, 1956. **DAN WEINER**

WAITING FOR RIDES AT A PICKUP POINT DURING THE
BOYCOTT. **DAN WEINER**

ABOVE: KING AND OTHER LEADERS OF THE
MONTGOMERY IMPROVEMENT ASSOCIATION (MIA)
CONTINUING DISCUSSIONS AFTER AN EXECUTIVE
BOARD MEETING AT THE MIA OFFICE, 1956.
DAN WEINER

In the background, left, is Rev. H. H. Hubbard, with
an unidentified man; in conversation with King (left) is
Rev. R. J. Glasco.

RIGHT: MARTIN LUTHER KING, JR., ADDRESSING
A MASS MEETING AT FIRST BAPTIST CHURCH DURING
THE BOYCOTT. DAN WEINER

"REV. KING FOUND GUILTY. The Rev. Martin Luther King Jr. got a big kiss from his wife today after Circuit Court Judge Eugene Carter found him guilty of a conspiracy to boycott Montgomery city busses. King was the first of 90 Negroes tried in the racial bus boycott. The judge fined him $500 and suspended the fine pending appeal. The other Negroes will not be tried at this time. King is free on bond." (Original AP caption.)

King's first book, *Stride toward Freedom: The Montgomery Story* (1958), was called "the handbook of the movement" because of the detailed information it contained about methods of nonviolent resistance. The book concludes:

This is a great hour for the Negro. The challenge is here. To become the instruments of a great idea is a privilege that history gives only occasionally. Arnold Toynbee says in *A Study of History* that it may be the Negro who will give the spiritual dynamic to Western civilization that it so desperately needs to survive. . . . Today the choice is no longer between violence and nonviolence. It is either nonviolence or nonexistence. The Negro may be God's appeal to this age—an age drifting rapidly to its doom. The eternal appeal takes the form of a warning: "All that live by the sword will perish by the sword."

ABOVE AND OPPOSITE: MARTIN LUTHER KING, JR.,
ARRESTED ON A LOITERING CHARGE, MONTGOMERY,
SEPTEMBER 3, 1958. **CHARLES MOORE**

King was trying to enter a crowded courtroom that was hearing a case involving his friend and colleague Ralph Abernathy. King was told to move on; when he didn't, he was arrested by two officers (who didn't recognize him). When Coretta Scott King tried to speak up, they threatened her: "Just nod your head and you'll go to jail too." They marched King down to police headquarters and shoved him against the desk. The sergeant handed over keys to a cell, as Coretta King looked on.

When King was convicted on the loitering charge, he elected to serve his sentence. Copies of his dramatic courtroom speech about the necessity of conscientious resistance were distributed to the press by Abernathy. King's protest

was aborted when his fine was paid by Police Commissioner Clyde Sellers, who told reporters that he was just saving the taxpayers' money and that King was only trying to promote his new book, *Stride toward Freedom: The Montgomery Story.*

Charles Moore, a staff photographer for the *Montgomery Advertiser,* was covering the Abernathy hearing when the un-expected arrest took place. His photographs were sent out worldwide through the Associated Press, triggering outrage and a flurry of financial support for the Montgomery Improvement Association.

2

LITTLE ROCK CENTRAL HIGH, 1957, AND THE UNIVERSITY OF MISSISSIPPI, 1962

"Don't Let Them See You Cry"

The dawn of 1957 held great promise for the civil rights movement. To build on the Montgomery victory, over forty ministers and other black leaders convened in Atlanta and formed the Southern Christian Leadership Conference. The SCLC would coordinate the efforts of many local church-based civil rights groups. With Martin Luther King, Jr., as its president, the SCLC would become the country's most powerful civil rights organization. King made the cover of *Time* magazine in February, which featured a story about the Montgomery boycott and its leader. He became the second African American ever to be interviewed on *Meet the Press.* In March, Martin and Coretta King were invited to Ghana (the first independent nation in sub-Saharan Africa) to celebrate its independence. King was impressed by the "intense democracy of the African Negro deriving from his tribal life"[1] and by the fact that Ghana's independence had been achieved nonviolently. He felt confirmed in his optimistic belief that the age was moving toward freedom. Indeed, by 1960 there would be seventeen new African states.

Yet in opposition to these triumphs there was much dark intransigence—notably, in the segregated schools of the South. In May 1954 the Supreme Court of the United States issued its decision on the case called *Oliver Brown et al. v. Board of Education of Topeka, Kansas.* The court ruled that separate-but-equal segregated schools violated the Fourteenth Amendment to the Constitution. Two weeks later they issued a ruling that school desegregation must take place "with all deliberate speed," a phrase whose vagueness would prove to be a major impediment to achieving integrated schools.

The white South's reaction to the *Brown v. Board* decisions ranged from token compliance to vehement refusal. Senator James Eastland of Mississippi, a leading spokesman

of the southern resistance, said that the Supreme Court was controlled by "pressure groups bent upon the destruction of the white race. . . . The Court has responded to a radical pro-Communist movement in this country. . . . We in the South cannot stay longer on the defensive. This is the road to destruction and death. We must take the offensive."[2] The Southern Manifesto of 1956 was signed by over one hundred congressmen from the southern states, who called the *Brown* decision unconstitutional and pledged to reverse it.

Just two months after the *Brown* decision the first White Citizens Council was formed—in Indianola, Mississippi, the seat of Senator Eastland's home county. Soon a network of over five hundred local councils throughout the South had enlisted tens of thousands of members. The councils and allied groups such as the National Association for the Advancement of White People and White America, Inc., were set up to intimidate integrationists and to give racism respectability. The citizens councils were like a Ku Klux Klan in suits rather than sheets (though council members sometimes carried their hoods in their briefcases).

Southern state legislatures started passing bills designed to prevent school integration, and local school boards followed suit; civil-court challenges to school integration proliferated. These obstructions were often countered by vigorous legal action on the part of the NAACP. In February 1956, for example, the NAACP helped Autherine Lucy enroll for graduate studies at the University of Alabama. When white mobs took to the streets in protest, the university expelled Lucy. The failure of the federal government to intervene sent the message that such resistance to integration could succeed.

In Birmingham, Alabama, the Reverend Fred Shuttlesworth tried to enroll two of his children in their neighborhood all-white high school. A waiting mob beat Shuttlesworth almost to death with metal chains, stabbed his wife, and attacked the Shuttlesworth children. The youngest child, Fred Junior, saw the brutal incident broadcast on the evening news. Farther west, in Little Rock, the capital of Arkansas, a battle was

SEE PAGE 129

PREVIOUS PAGE: ELIZABETH ECKFORD, ONE OF THE LITTLE ROCK NINE, PURSUED BY THE MOB OUTSIDE LITTLE ROCK CENTRAL HIGH SCHOOL, SEPTEMBER 4, 1957. **PETE HARRIS**

Melba Patillo Beals, another of the Little Rock Nine, has written:

> In the Sunday paper, I saw a pitiful closeup photograph of Elizabeth, walking alone in front of Central on the first day of integration. It pained my insides to see, once again, the twisted scowling faces with open mouths jeering, clustered around my friend's head like bouquets of grotesque flowers. It was an ad paid for by a white man from a small town in Arkansas. "If you live in Arkansas," the ad read, "study this picture and know shame. When hate is unleashed and bigotry finds a voice, God help us all."
>
> I felt a kind of joy and hope in the thought that one white man was willing to use his own money to call attention to the injustice we were facing. Maybe the picture would help others realize that what they were doing was hurting everybody.

commencing that would raise the ghost of the War Between the States and that would focus the eyes of the world on an American disgrace.

Little Rock was considered to be a relatively liberal southern metropolis, with some integration of its libraries, parks, buses, and even residential neighborhoods and the police force. The school board of Little Rock had been the first in the South to issue a statement of compliance with the *Brown v. Board* decision. Their plan called for admitting a token group of black students to Little Rock Central High School, an academically outstanding, well-equipped modern school with over two thousand white students, whose castlelike edifice was considered the most beautiful high school building in America. There was reason to believe that the token integration of Central High would proceed smoothly.

But on Labor Day night, 1957, Arkansas Governor Orval Faubus went on television to announce that he was surrounding Central High with the National Guard. "They will not act as segregationists or integrationists, but as soldiers called to active duty to carry out their assigned tasks. But I must state here in all sincerity that it is my opinion, yes, even conviction, that it will not be possible to restore or maintain order and protect the lives and property of the citizens if forcible integration is carried out tomorrow in the schools of this community."[3] Faubus had decided that taking this stand would secure his reelection later that year.

Melba Patillo was one of the nine black students who were ready to integrate Central High the next day. She watched the Faubus broadcast with her family. "The Governor has finally flipped his wig," her mother, Lois, commented. "He's stirring up trouble by talking about trouble," was the prophetic comment of her grandmother India.[4] When Governor Faubus marshaled his National Guard he raised the school-desegregation conflict to a new level. The politicians' posturings, the legislative impediments, the civil suits, the individual and organized acts of intimidation and terrorism were now being reinforced by armed might under the command of a state executive.

The Little Rock Nine intended to enter Central High in spite of it all. They were Minniejean Brown, Elizabeth Eckford, Ernest Green, Thelma Mothershed, Melba Patillo, Gloria Ray, Terrance Roberts, Jefferson Thomas, and Carlotta Walls, aged fourteen to sixteen. They were guided by Daisy Bates, president of the Arkansas NAACP. Bates and her husband, L. C. Bates, published the *Arkansas State Press,* the local black newsweekly (circulation of about twenty thousand). Daisy Bates was the liaison between the nine children and the school board. The first day of school, she had the children meet at her home before driving to school as a group.

But Elizabeth Eckford, who had no telephone at home, did not know about the meeting. She did know that the school board had requested that her parents not accompany her. She donned a starched black-and-white dress sewn especially for that day. She rode a public bus to school alone. Outside Central High, Elizabeth found herself between a chain of armed guards and a large, cursing white mob. Not one other black face was to be seen. She held back her panic as she rushed to the school's front entrance.

> I stood looking at the school—it looked so big! Just then the guards let some white students through. The crowd was quiet. I guess they were waiting to see what was going to happen. When I was able to steady my knees, I walked up to the guard who had let the white students in. He didn't move. When I tried to squeeze past him, he raised his bayonet and then the other guards moved in and they raised their bayonets. They glared at me with a mean look and I was very frightened and didn't know what to do. I turned around and the crowd came toward me. They moved closer and closer. Somebody started yelling, "Lynch her! Lynch her!"[5]

Eckford fled to a bus-stop bench as a small island of safety, but the mob continued to harass her. One reporter stepped up for an interview. *New York Times* education writer Benjamin Fine comforted her, saying, "Don't let them see you cry." A white woman named Grace Lorch finally guided Elizabeth to the safety of an approaching bus that took her home.

For the next two weeks the Little Rock Nine studied at home while Faubus clashed with the U.S. Justice Department and other federal authorities. President Dwight D. Eisenhower, who had been reluctant to intervene, summoned Faubus to his Newport, Rhode Island, summer residence to tell him that he must comply. After a court order Faubus went on television again, this time to announce the complete withdrawal of his troops, to be replaced by—Faubus didn't say what. He flew to Georgia to attend a southern governors' conference and a football game. Faubus was considered a hero by the southern intransigents. "He's really lapping up the glory. There were 33,000 people at the game, and every time they cheered a play, Faubus stood up and bowed," a fellow governor was quoted saying in *Time*.[6]

The nine black children approached Central High together on Monday, September 23, accompanied by a small contingent of city policemen. They were slipped in through a side door. The reaction of the waiting mob was described in a dispatch by Benjamin Fine:

> The crowd let out a roar of rage. "They've gone in," a man shouted. "Oh, God," said a woman, "the niggers are in school." A group of six girls, dressed in skirts and sweaters, hair in pony-tails, started to shriek and wail. "The niggers are in our school," they howled hysterically. One of them jumped up and down on the sidewalk, waving her arms toward her classmates in the school who were looking out of the windows, and screamed over and over again: "Come on out, come on out." Tears flowed down her face, her body shook in uncontrollable spasms. . . . Hysteria swept from the shrieking girls to members of the crowd.[7]

Inside the school, the nine were separated. When they protested, they were told, "You want integration, you'll get integration." Recalling that moment of going off alone, Melba Patillo wrote, "There has never been in my life any stark terror or any fear akin to that."[8]

The mob soon took control of the school, both inside and out. The nine, under threat of death, were frantically shepherded to the principal's office. Melba overheard officials conferring in the adjoining room: "We may have to let the mob have one of those kids, so's we can distract them long enough to get the others out." "They're children. What'll we do, have them draw straws to see which one gets a rope around their neck?"[9] Assistant Chief of Police Gene Smith took charge and hurried the frightened students into the basement garage. They were hustled into two cars and told to keep their heads down. Smith told the drivers, "Move fast and don't stop no matter what." The cars sped up a ramp and through the waiting mob, escaping without injuries.

The September 23 riot at Central High was broadcast across the nation and made headline news around the world. From Georgia, Faubus declared: "The trouble in Little Rock vindicates my good judgment." Daisy Bates declared that the children would not return to Central until the president himself assured their safety. Little Rock's mayor, Woodrow Mann, twice requested that federal troops be deployed to guard them. Finally, Eisenhower gave the order that sent federal troops into the South to protect black citizens for the first time since Reconstruction.

Another first: Melba Patillo was allowed to take a dinner tray to the television so that she could hear the president's televised address. "He is our President, and he happens to be talking about us," Grandmother India declared. "The whole world's watching, why shouldn't we."[10]

Eisenhower explained his reluctant intervention in legalistic and geopolitical terms:

> Under the leadership of demagogic extremists, disorderly mobs have deliberately prevented the carrying out of proper orders from a federal court. . . . Whenever normal agencies prove inadequate to the task and it becomes necessary for the executive branch of the federal government to use its powers and authority to uphold federal courts, the President's responsibility is inescapable. . . . At a time when we face grave situations at home and abroad because of the hatred that communism bears towards a system of government based on human rights, it would be difficult to exaggerate the harm that is being done to the prestige and influence, and indeed the safety, of our nation and the world.[11]

Eisenhower ordered more than one thousand members of the renowned 101st Airborne Division to fly in, fully armed, from Fort Campbell, Kentucky. The "Screaming Eagles" had earned their reputation at the Battle of the Bulge, a turning point in World War II. Eisenhower also federalized the Arkansas National Guard, taking over their command from Faubus, and ordered them to support the integration.

That night Melba Patillo slept in pajamas for the first time in a long time—instead of the street clothes she had been wearing to bed to be ready for the attacks being threatened by hate calls and letters. When she woke up the next morning, she found Grandma India asleep with her rifle on her lap.

The Little Rock Nine gathered yet again at Daisy Bates's house for their third attempt to study at Central High. This time they drove to school in a heavily armed convoy. Ernest Green, the eldest of the nine and the only senior, remembers: "When we got to the front of the school, the whole school was ringed with paratroopers and helicopters hovering around, and we marched up the steps with this circle of soldiers with bayonets drawn. Walking up the steps that day was probably one of the biggest feelings I've ever had, I figured I had finally cracked it."[12]

That was a school year of "hand-to-hand combat . . . trench warfare," as Green describes it.[13] At first, each of the nine was assigned a soldier from the 101st as his or her personal guard. But after a week the army troops were withdrawn, and security fell to the much less vigilant nationalized Alabama Guardsmen. Most of their classmates ostracized the black students and subjected them to taunts, physical abuse, and continuous threats. They were hanged and burned in effigy. Melba Patillo was almost blinded by a chemical thrown at her eyes.

The Little Rock Nine kept their sanity through prayer and togetherness. Melba was given a book about Gandhi and found its teachings about nonviolence helpful. There were no mass meetings or freedom songs, but there were interviews, photographs, and court hearings to help the students feel that their struggle was important. There were lots of jokes and group study sessions. Together they learned "readin', writin' and riotin'."

One afternoon Minniejean Brown, a large girl, was in the lunch line. She could stand the taunts of "nigger, nigger, nigger" no longer and dumped a bowl of chili on her tormentor's head. The all-black lunchroom staff broke into applause. After Minniejean was suspended, and eventually expelled, from Central High, a printed card circulated among the white students, "One down, eight to go." With the help of Daisy Bates and Dr. Kenneth Clark, whose testimony had been so important to the *Brown v. Board* decision, Minniejean was able to complete her studies at New Lincoln School in New York City.

Eight of the nine made it through the term. That spring Ernest Green became the first African American to graduate from Little Rock Central High. Martin Luther King, Jr., attended the graduation ceremony.

Faubus continued to preach against integration and won an unprecedented third term as governor. In 1958 he closed the Little Rock public schools entirely. A Gallup poll from that time showed Faubus as one of the ten men most admired in America, on a list with Albert Schweitzer, Jonas Salk, General Douglas MacArthur, and President Eisenhower. Not until two years later were the schools reopened, on orders of the U.S. Supreme Court. By 1964 only 123 black children out of 7,000 were attending desegregated schools in Little Rock.

SEE PAGE 60

In 1961, seven years after *Brown v. Board*, there was still not a single integrated public school or institution of higher learning in the state of Mississippi. A lone black student, James Meredith, decided to break down those barriers in his home state. Meredith heard in President John F. Kennedy's 1961 inauguration speech a call for all Americans to struggle for freedom around the globe. The next morning Meredith applied for admittance to the University of Mississippi. In a statement explaining his decision he wrote:

> We have a dilemma. It is a fact that the Negroes of Mississippi are effectively not first-class citizens. I feel that every citizen should be a first-class citizen and should be allowed to develop his talents on a free, equal, and competitive basis. . . . I dream of a day when Negroes in Mississippi can live in decency and respect and do so without fear of intimidation and bodily harm, of receiving personal embarrassment, and with an assurance of equal justice under the law.[14]

With the help of the NAACP and its leader in Mississippi, Medgar Evers, Meredith fought a barrage of legal challenges to his application for admission. Finally, a federal court order in September 1962 enjoined the university's registrar from further obstruction. At that point Governor Ross Barnett had himself declared emergency registrar and physically barred Meredith's approach to the registration desk. This stance greatly boosted Barnett's popularity (which had been suffering from a scandal over the gold-plated faucets that he'd had installed in the governor's residence). In a televised speech Barnett said: " There is no case in history where the Caucasian race has survived social integration. . . . We must either submit to the unlawful dictate of the federal government or stand up like men and tell them 'Never.'"[15] "Never" became the rallying cry of the Ole Miss segregationists. A song was penned, "Never, No Never." Meredith, accompanied by Justice Department officials, had his attempts to register rebuffed four times by Barnett and by Lieutenant Governor Paul Johnson.

U.S. Attorney General Robert F. Kennedy and President Kennedy were pressuring Barnett to back down; Barnett countered by wheedling the Kennedys into staging a show of force. When negotiations faltered over exactly how many guns would be drawn in the charade, the Kennedys threatened public exposure of those negotiations, an exposure that would have meant Barnett's political ruin in a state where a favorite football-crowd chant was, "Ask us what we say, it's to hell with Bobby K."

An ugly mob two thousand strong was forming on campus, with defenders of Ole Miss pouring in from many states, armed with beer coolers, Confederate flags, and rifles. President Kennedy authorized the deployment of army troops (after first asking, "Is this pretty much what Ike signed in 1957 with the Little Rock thing?"[16]). Meanwhile, Barnett proposed another plan: sneak Meredith on campus and register him a day ahead of schedule so that Barnett could claim he had been tricked by the Feds. The Kennedys agreed to this latest ruse, held back the army, and patched together a civilian force of

SEE PAGE 62

border patrolmen, federal prison guards, and federal marshals (tax men, lawyers, and whoever else could be found around the Justice Department that Sunday).

The federal force was deployed around the university's administration building, called the Lyceum. The rowdies chanted hate slogans and taunted the marshals. Meredith was flown into Oxford and hidden in a dormitory building. He read and studied quietly; the guards at his door had orders to kill anyone who tried to get in. As darkness descended, a battle commenced at the Lyceum. Rocks, bottles, and lead pipes were thrown at the marshals. Cars and windows were smashed. Barnett's contingent of state highway patrolmen was pulled out. Molotov cocktails were thrown and guns fired. A London *Daily Sketch* reporter, Paul Guihard, was shot dead at close range. Marshals were wounded with shotguns and high-powered-rifle bullets.

Around 10:00 P.M. the attorney general was told, "Bob, I'm very sorry to report we've had to fire the tear gas. We had no choice."[17] President Kennedy returned from giving a televised speech on the confrontation to find the situation so dangerous that the army would have to be called in after all. During the four hours it took to deploy the troops, the marshals suffered the majority of the 160 injuries and the 28 gunshot wounds that they would sustain that night. It was 4:30 A.M. before the riot was quelled. The soldiers arrested over two hundred people, only one-quarter of them Ole Miss students.

At 9:00 A.M., Meredith sat down to his first class, Colonial American History. Troops stayed on to guard him until the end of the term, when he graduated with a bachelor's degree in political science. On his graduation gown he wore a "Never" button pinned upside down.

Reactions to the battle at Ole Miss were many. Some civil rights activists took pleasure in a victory won—and in Mississippi, the toughest state of all. Many Mississippi blacks relished the victory, too. But Martin Luther King, Jr., was depressed by the Barnett-Kennedy dealing and scheming, saying it "made Negroes feel like pawns in a white man's political game."[18] The rest of the nation was shocked by what they saw on television and in the press. It had been five years since the integration battle at Central High, yet in Mississippi, at least, no lessons had been learned.

LINDA BROWN AND HER SISTER WALKING TO SCHOOL, TOPEKA, KANSAS, MARCH 1953.
CARL IWASAKI

On May 17, 1954, the Supreme Court ruled on *Oliver Brown et al. v. the Board of Education of Topeka, Kansas* and ended legal public-school segregation in the United States. The case was named for the father of fourth-grader Linda Brown—seen here at age ten, with her sister Terry Lynn, age six. Under segregation laws they were not allowed to attend nearby New Summer School but had to walk six blocks through the dangerous Rock Island Switchyard in order to catch a bus to all-black Monroe School.

THE LITTLE ROCK NINE, SEPTEMBER 13, 1957.
CHET WOZNEY

"Little Rock Nine Study on Their Own—The nine Negro students who were prevented from entering Little Rock Central High School are shown after having formed a study circle of their own. Not having enrolled elsewhere at school, they will be assigned a tutor next week. From left, they are: (seated on floor) Thelma Mothershed, Elizabeth Eckford, and Melba Patillo. (Seated above) Jefferson Thomas, Ernest Green, Minnie Jean [sic] Brown, Carlotta Walls, Terence [sic] Roberts, and Gloria Ray." (Original UPI caption.)

THE LITTLE ROCK NINE ENTER CENTRAL HIGH UNDER
ARMED GUARD, SEPTEMBER 25, 1957. **BURT GLINN**

Elizabeth Huckaby, the assistant principal for girls at Central, has written:

> I imagine that I have seen hundreds of pictures of the black students escorted by the 101st into Central High school. These pictures all show the Nine walking up the front steps. But none is the picture as I saw it from the lobby. Through the open doors at the far side of the lobby came a double file of nine black children, with a protec-
>
> tive line of fully armed guards on each side of them. . . . They paused at the center of the lobby . . . while a photographer from the 101st took the official picture. . . . [Principal] Jess Matthews stepped forward. "Well, good morning, boys and girls; this is the first class period, and you all know your way to that class. You may go to class, now," he said.

ABOVE: LAW OFFICERS GATHERED AT THE UNIVERSITY
OF MISSISSIPPI, OXFORD, SEPTEMBER 1962.
CHARLES MOORE

Local police fervently supported Governor Ross Barnett's
refusal to admit James Meredith as the first black student
at "Ole Miss." Here, one officer practices his billy club
swings while another prepares identifying armbands.

While he was shooting this story, Moore's hotel room
was invaded by a pack of angry students. One of them
began to choke Moore and shout obscenities in his face.
Moore recalls: "I never took my eyes off his eyes. I have
never seen such hate on anyone's face before; it was as if I
were vermin. I knew what he was thinking. To him I was
worse than 'a nigger,' I was a white nigger. . . . And worse
than that I was a white *Life* magazine nigger.'"

OPPOSITE: **UNITED PRESS INTERNATIONAL**

"TWO KILLED IN RIOT, Oxford, Miss.: Students, one of
them waving a Confederate flag, shout insults at U.S. marshals who surrounded the administration building at the
University of Mississippi late Sept. 30th to await the
arrival of Negro James Meredith. Later, under cover of
darkness, Meredith was ushered into a campus dormitory
by a guard of 15 marshals. Then the demonstration outside
the university exploded into a full-scale riot. Two persons
were killed and 75 injured before the crowds were routed
from the campus with tear gas and bayonets." (Original
UPI caption.)

OPPOSITE, TOP: AN EXHAUSTED AND INJURED MARSHAL COLLAPSES IN THE HALLWAY OF THE BESIEGED ADMINISTRATION BUILDING, UNIVERSITY OF MISSISSIPPI, SEPTEMBER 30, 1962. **CHARLES MOORE**

OPPOSITE, BOTTOM: SOLDIERS GUARDING ARRESTED RIOTERS, UNIVERSITY OF MISSISSIPPI, OCTOBER 1, 1962. **CHARLES MOORE**

ABOVE: JAMES MEREDITH, ACCOMPANIED BY FEDERAL OFFICIALS, REGISTERS AT THE UNIVERSITY OF MISSISSIPPI, OCTOBER 1, 1962. **CHARLES MOORE**

Meredith is front and center; at left is Chief U.S. Marshal James McShane; on the right is John Doar, first assistant in the Justice Department's Civil Rights Division.

3

SIT-INS AND FREEDOM RIDES, 1960–62

"This Was the Answer"

On Monday, the first of February, 1960, four black college freshman, four friends, sat down at the sixty-six-seat F. W. Woolworth's lunch counter in Greensboro, North Carolina. They ordered coffee and doughnuts. The waitress said, "I'm sorry, we don't serve you here." They argued that they should be served, that the other counters in the store had been happy to take their money, they showed receipts to prove it.

A policeman—who arrived on the scene by chance—paced behind the four youths, slapping his billy club in his hand, not sure what to do and red-faced with consternation. The smooth store manager tried to talk them off their seats. The four politely refused, and the manager took no action. They sat, unserved, until closing time, their fear turning into confidence, then joy. Franklin McCain remembered: "I probably felt better on that day than I've ever felt in my life. Seems like a lot of feelings of guilt or what-have-you suddenly left me, and I felt as though I had gained my manhood, so to speak, and not only gained it, but had developed quite a lot of respect for it."[1]

News of their sortie beat the four freshmen back to campus. They met with enthusiastic student leaders and organized a follow-up protest; it put thirty students at the same Woolworth's lunch counter the next day. The day after that, so many black students (joined by some whites) were sitting in that they seriously disrupted downtown commerce. Economic pressure had been added to moral persuasion. By the end of the week Greensboro's mayor had requested and received a two-week cease-fire to negotiate the students' demands.

Within two weeks, sit-ins were mounted in eight North Carolina communities and in Virginia. By the end of February, thirty-one communities in seven states had sit-ins.

The demonstrations spread to all of the southern states by mid-April, with 50,000–70,000 protesters taking part. The explosion of direct-action protest that would be called "the Movement" had been ignited. "The Sixties" had begun.

Since their arrival that autumn at all-black North Carolina Agricultural and Technical College, Ezell Blair, Jr., Franklin McCain, Joseph McNeil, and David Richmond had become a tight circle of friends. In their bull sessions they often argued over what to do about the daily pain inflicted on them by the local segregation laws. They were all members of NAACP Youth Councils; they knew about the sit-ins that the attorney Floyd McKissick and Rev. Douglas Moore had been staging in nearby Durham over the last three years. After goading each other to take some action, to do something, the four freshmen had come up with the Woolworth's sit-in plan on the Sunday night just before they tried it out.

Since 1957 there had been sit-ins organized in at least sixteen cities in the upper South and in the Deep South. Why did the one in Greensboro stir up so many followers? Some of the reasons are evident. Unlike almost all previous sit-ins, this one was not sponsored by any organization. The four freshmen had the most minimal of plans, the vaguest of goals. Their spontaneous action elicited not brutal repression, but dumbfoundedness; they were not jailed or beaten—they were left to sit. When their friends and colleagues heard what had happened, they needed no explanations, no long discussions or debates. They had been brought up on *Brown v. Board*, on the Montgomery bus boycott, on Little Rock Central High. This was what they had been waiting for; they clamored to join in. It seemed so easy, like a miracle of success.

Less miraculous was how the sit-ins quickly spread to other locales. There were ten black colleges within a few miles of Greensboro. North Carolina's dense network of black student associations, civil rights groups, and churches buzzed with the news and quickly supported and extended the Greensboro actions. A command center in nearby

PREVIOUS PAGE: SIT-IN AT F. W. WOOLWORTH'S LUNCH COUNTER, JACKSON, MISSISSIPPI, MAY 28, 1963. **FRED BLACKWELL**

Inspired by the successes of the Birmingham movement, Medgar Evers and other Mississippi NAACP leaders decided to step up direct-action protests in Jackson. The press and police were given advance notice of actions scheduled for the morning of May 28, when Anne Moody (seen at the counter, on the right) led a group of Tougaloo College students in a sit-in at Woolworth's. At exactly 11:15 A.M., Moody, Memphis Norman, and Pearlena Lewis sat down and requested service. The waitresses, white patrons, and police left them to the mercies of a lunchtime crowd of Jackson Central High students and downtown workers. They were taunted, beaten, wrenched from their seats, kicked, and thrown around the store. Salt, pepper, and ketchup were poured on their wounds. They were joined by other protesters, including white Tougaloo student Joan Trumpauer (seated next to Moody) and Tougaloo social science professor John Salter, an NAACP stalwart (next to Trumpauer). The beatings went on for over three hours before the store was closed and the demonstrators removed by police. "After the sit-in, all I could think about was how sick Mississippi whites were," Moody would write.

Durham was set up by McKissick (an NAACP associate), by Rev. Moore (associated with the SCLC), and by Gordon Carey (a white CORE field secretary). Within a week after the first Greensboro sit-in, they had organized students from several local colleges, shuttling them from campus to church to lunch counters for a coordinated, multisite sit-in.

This cooperative effort was typical of the sit-in movement: the troops were housed on campuses, but black churches were the training and staging centers. The students had the impatience, the bravery, the time, and the energy to put themselves on the front lines. The churches and civil rights groups provided experienced organizers and the resources for communications, transportation, legal aid, and other such essentials. The SCLC—an alignment of church-based groups committed to nonviolent direct action—was a particularly important activist network.

By the third day of the Greensboro sit-ins, Rev. Moore in Durham was eager for the momentum to spread to other states. He telephoned his friend the Reverend James Lawson, in Nashville, to ask if Lawson was ready. Moore knew that Lawson had been planning sit-ins in Nashville and had led "test sit-ins" at two lunch counters before the Christmas holidays. Like Greensboro, Nashville had a complex of black institutions that would support protests.

Lawson, thirty years old, was a black divinity student at Vanderbilt University. He had been jailed for his pacifist objections to the Korean War, then paroled on the recognizance of Methodist ministers who sent him to India as a missionary. There Lawson studied Gandhian passive resistance. During the Montgomery boycott he had tutored Martin Luther King, Jr., in Gandhi's philosophy, methods, and achievements. Afterward, working for the Fellowship of Reconciliation (FOR), Lawson conducted workshops in nonviolence in student centers throughout the South. Many important movement leaders were trained in those workshops.

The Nashville student movement, tutored in Lawson's Tuesday night Nashville workshops, marshaled over five hundred students for its first sit-ins, on February 18. The Nashville movement would steam on for months, the largest and best organized of all the sit-in movements. It garnered extraordinary media attention and seasoned many civil rights activists.

On Friday, February 26, Nashville's chief of police announced that, at the request of store owners, he would begin to arrest demonstrators. Student leader John Lewis stayed up all that night to write and mimeograph a last-minute list of basic instructions. "Do show yourself friendly on the counter at all times. Do sit straight and always face the counter. Don't strike back, or curse if attacked. Don't laugh out. Don't hold conversations. Don't block entrances."[2] The list ended: "Remember the teachings of Jesus, Gandhi, Thoreau, and Martin Luther King, Jr."[3]

The next day the sit-in students were harassed and attacked by white thugs, yanked from their stools, punched and kicked—with the connivance of the police. The demonstrators held to their tenets of nonviolence. Eighty-two demonstrators—seventy-seven black, five white—were arrested for "disorderly conduct." After their conviction the student leader Diane Nash, Lewis, and almost all of the others refused their fines, opting instead to brave the jail cells. This strategy would be called "jail—no bail." As longtime organizer Bayard Rustin explained in the *Student Voice:* "There are not enough jails to accommodate the movement. This is an important strength. If one or two of us are arrested, the rest must non-violently seek arrest. If, upon arrest, you pay your bail or fine, you provide room for a friend. Only so many can fit into a cell; if you remain here, there can be no more arrests! Imprisonment is an expense to the state; it must feed and take care of you. Bails and fines are an expense to the movement, which it can ill afford."[4]

Nashville's black community raised the necessary legal funds and found another way to support the students: a strangling boycott of downtown businesses. Not since Montgomery had there been such an effective boycott, and this one was much broader than just buses. It soon had downtown merchants seeking a settlement.

At 5:30 A.M. on April 19 a devastating bomb exploded in the Nashville house of Alexander Looby, a prominent black attorney who was representing the arrested students. Looby and his family escaped the ruins without serious injury. By noon hundreds of protesters had gathered in the streets to march on city hall—the first major march of the civil rights movement. Rev. C. T. Vivian, a leading activist minister, recalls:

> We walked by a place where there were workers out for the noon hour, white workers. And they had never seen anything like this. And here was all of 4,000 people marching down the street, and all you could hear was their feet as we silently moved. And they didn't know what to do. And they moved back up against the wall, and they simply stood against the wall, just looking. There was a fear there, there was an awe, and they did not know what to do. But they knew that this was not to be stopped, this was not to be played with, or to be joked with.[5]

Mayor Ben West met the marchers on the city hall steps, where he listened to Vivian condemn the mayor's inaction. Then, as television cameras recorded the confrontation, Diane Nash asked the mayor if he felt that discrimination on the basis of race was wrong. "As a man had to answer, not a politician," West said he did think it wrong. "Mayor Says Integrate Counters," a headline announced the next day. Three weeks later the first Nashville lunch counters began serving blacks alongside whites.[6]

The sit-ins, whether seen firsthand or brought home via newspapers or television, transformed the way many white southerners saw themselves and their black neighbors. An onlooker in Atlanta exclaimed, "I didn't know there were that many niggers *in* college."[7] Yolande Fox, an Alabaman who had been Miss America, explained why she joined a sympathy picket of Woolworth's in New York City. "I'm a Southern girl, but I'm a thinking girl."[8] The *Greensboro Daily News* commented: "There are many white people in the

South who recognize the injustice of the lunch counter system. It is based on circumstances which may have made sense 100 years ago; today it has a touch of medievalism. It smacks of Indian 'untouchables' or Hitlerian Master Race Theories."[9] The segregationist *Richmond News Leader* editorialized on February 22:

> Many a Virginian must have felt a tinge of wry regret at the state of things as they are, in reading of Saturday's "sit-downs" by Negro students in Richmond stores. Here were the colored students, in coats, white shirts, ties, and one of them was reading Goethe and one was taking notes from a biology text. And here, on the sidewalk outside, was a gang of white boys come to heckle, a ragtail rabble, slack-jawed, black-jacketed, grinning fit to kill, and some of them, God save the mark, were waving the proud and honored flag of the Southern States.[10]

SEE PAGE 78

Young African Americans, north and south, were transfixed by images of the sit-ins and through them discovered new hopes and new selves. Ruby Doris Smith, a student at Atlanta's Spelman College, rushed home each day to watch broadcasts of the sit-ins and imagined them coming to her hometown.[11] Cleveland Sellers, a high school senior in Denmark, South Carolina, would catch the evening news at the student union:

> With the exception of the announcer's voice, the lounge would be so quiet you could hear a rat pissing on cotton. Hundreds of thoughts coursed through my head as I stood with my eyes transfixed on the television screen. My identification with the demonstrating students was so thorough that I would flinch every time one of the whites taunted them. On nights when I saw the picture of students being beaten and dragged through the streets by their hair, I would leave the lounge in a rage.[12]

Robert Moses, a twenty-six-year-old math teacher at New York's Horace Mann High School, was stunned by a photograph that captured the "sullen, angry, determined" look of the student protesters. "Before, the Negro in the South had always looked on the defensive, cringing. This time they were taking the initiative. They were kids my age, and I knew this had something to do with my own life. It made me realize that for a long time I had been troubled by the problem of being a Negro and at the same time being an American. This was the answer."[13] Smith, Sellers, and Moses would all become important members of SNCC.

The sit-ins in Atlanta in October influenced the nation in a different way. The students laid out a strategy designed to illuminate the tepid support of the civil rights movement by presidential candidates Richard Nixon and John F. Kennedy. Martin Luther King, Jr., had moved from Montgomery to Atlanta to share with his father the pastorship of Ebenezer Baptist Church. According to plan, he was arrested as a sit-in participant just two weeks before election day. On a technicality involving probation for a traffic violation, King was sentenced to four months in a Georgia penitentiary. Senator and presidential candidate Kennedy called Coretta Scott King, offering his concern and his help. He pressured Alabama and Georgia officials to release King, who was subsequently bailed out. The ensuing support of Kennedy by black ministers in Sunday-before-the-election sermons and by black voters has been widely cited as a force that made the crucial difference in securing Kennedy's extremely close victory.

Days after the first Greensboro sit-in, Fred Shuttlesworth had gone to nearby High Point, North Carolina, to give a guest sermon. After witnessing a demonstration by High Point students, he excitedly telephoned Ella Baker, executive director of the SCLC office in Atlanta. "You must tell Martin that we must get with this." He felt that these sit-ins might "shake up the world."[14] Having secured eight hundred dollars from SCLC, Baker invited student activists to a conference to be held in Raleigh over Easter weekend, April 15–17.

Two weeks before that conference, the first conference of student activists was convened by Septima Clark at the Highlander Folk School in rural Tennessee. Over eighty student leaders showed up to discuss the sit-in movement and where it was going. Highlander, where Rosa Parks had studied in 1955, was what historian Aldon Morris calls a "movement halfway house." Highlander, the Fellowship of Reconciliation, the American Friends Service Committee, the Southern Conference Educational Fund, the War Resisters League, and others were small organizations without a mass base that nurtured the expanding movements of the 1960s. They provided theories of social change as well as places to meet, contact with experienced activists, and access to the media and to progressive philanthropy.[15]

SEE PAGE 40

For many of the students gathered at Highlander, the conference was their introduction to the "freedom songs" that would become such an important motivating force in the movement. Based at Highlander, Zilphia Horton, Guy Carawan, Pete Seeger, and others collected and adapted slave songs, gospel songs, folk songs, labor songs, and new songs, and taught them to the young activists. Movement participants began gathering and writing their own songs. "Keep Your Eyes on the Prize," "We Shall Not Be Moved," "This Little Light of Mine," and many others passed through Highlander and then out into the movement. "We Shall Overcome," an old song that had done service in the labor movement and elsewhere, became the particular anthem of the civil rights movement—and of successive movements around the world. It became a ritual to close movement gatherings with a rendition of "We Shall Overcome," sung with arms crossed, hands linked, bodies rocking from side to side. Time and again, the brave words and steady rhythm of the song fostered courage, unity, and hope.

For the Raleigh conference one hundred students were expected but about three hundred students and observers showed up, along with established leaders like Martin Luther King, Jr. Ella Baker—who was concerned that the brazen energy of the students might be smothered under the wing of the SCLC—pushed the students to form a separate, radically democratic organization that would be a loose confederation of coordinated local action groups. Heeding Baker's vision, they formed the Temporary Student Nonviolent Coordinating Committee.

James Lawson gave the most influential speech of the conference. He stressed that the goal was (in Baker's phrase) "bigger than a hamburger," bigger than integrated lunch counters and buses and stores. The prize would be no less than a spiritual rejuvenation of America. Lawson guided the drafting of the SNCC "Statement of Purpose" of May 14 (reprinted here in full):

> We affirm the philosophical or religious ideal of nonviolence as the foundation of our purpose, the presupposition of our faith, and the manner of our action. Nonviolence as it grows from the Judaic-Christian tradition seeks a social order of justice permeated by love. Integration of human endeavor represents the crucial first step towards such a society.
>
> Through nonviolence, courage displaces fear; love transforms hate. Acceptance dissipates prejudice; hope ends despair. Peace dominates war; faith reconciles doubt. Mutual regard cancels enmity. Justice for all overthrows injustice. The redemptive community supersedes systems of gross immorality.
>
> Love is the central motif of nonviolence. Love is the force by which God binds man to Himself and man to man. Such love goes to the extreme; it remains loving and forgiving even in the midst of hostility. It matches the capacity of evil to inflict suffering with an even more enduring capacity to absorb evil, all the while persisting in love.
>
> By appealing to the conscience and standing on the moral nature of human existence, nonviolence nurtures the atmosphere in which reconciliation and justice become actual possibilities.

By May of 1960 SNCC had dropped "Temporary" from its name, had been given a corner of the SCLC office in Atlanta as its first headquarters, and was establishing itself as the avant-garde of the civil rights movement.

The "Freedom Ride" was designed to be a Trojan horse of nonviolent action: a select cadre of commandos would be wheeled into the enemy camp in order to open the door to a larger force. For years to come, in some parts of the South, local blacks would respectfully call civil rights workers "Freedom Riders," while segregationist whites would use the phrase as a contemptuous taunt, perhaps joined to the accusation "Kennedy is your God."

Just days after the inauguration of President Kennedy in January 1961, James Farmer became national director of CORE and organized the first Freedom Ride. In 1947 CORE had tested a new Supreme Court ruling that outlawed segregated seating on interstate buses by sending an integrated group on a dangerous bus ride through the upper

South. In December 1960 the Supreme Court ruled that interstate bus terminals must also be desegregated. CORE initiated the Freedom Ride to test the new ruling and to test the new administration.

The Freedom Riders wanted to hold the new president to his campaign promises. Kennedy had vowed to end racial discrimination in public housing projects "with the stroke of a pen." After his election thousands of pens were sent to remind him, but no ink was spent. Kennedy made encouraging speeches and several heartening black appointments, but he backed no legislation that would seriously rile southern congressmen. Farmer said: "What we had to do was make it more dangerous politically for the federal government *not* to enforce federal law than it would be for them to enforce federal law. . . . We decided the way to do it was to have an interracial group ride through the South. . . . We felt we could count on the racists of the South to create a crisis so that the federal government would be compelled to enforce the law."[16]

In May 1961 thirteen volunteers gathered in Washington, D.C., to begin the journey. John Lewis, who joined the ride after seeing an ad in SNCC's *Student Voice,* remembers that on the eve of departure he tasted his first Chinese food, mixed with fear. The riders expected extreme violence; some had written letters to be posted in event of their death. The attorney general and the FBI were notified of their itinerary, as were the media.

Two groups set out, one on a Trailways bus, one on a Greyhound. They made it through Virginia, the Carolinas, and Georgia without any devastating attacks. Punishment arrived in Alabama. The Greyhound bus was surrounded in the Anniston bus depot by a large armed mob screaming at the riders to come out. Instead, the bus sped out of town, pursued by about fifty vehicles. Because the tires had been slashed by the mob, the driver was forced to pull over. The windows were smashed one by one, and the mob tried to pull out the terrified passengers. Then a firebomb was thrown in and the exits barred; the suffocating passengers managed to escape only after a state investigator on the bus fired warning shots from his revolver. State troopers arrived and broke up beatings in progress, as the bus burned to a skeleton. The wounded riders were later besieged at Anniston Hospital. Before they could be evicted by the frightened staff, they were rescued again, this time by a convoy of armed churchmen that had been dispatched from Birmingham by Fred Shuttlesworth.

Meanwhile, the Trailways riders were brutally beaten in the Anniston depot—to the point that one thug warned another to stop before he killed someone. That bus managed to drive on to the Birmingham station, where it was attacked by a group of Klansmen. According to Klan member and FBI informant Gary Thomas Rowe, the police had agreed to allow fifteen minutes of uninterrupted beating—a plan the FBI did nothing to stop. James Peck, the Peck & Peck Clothier heir who had also been on the 1947 test bus ride, was particularly savaged, requiring hospitalization and fifty stitches to six head wounds. Peck, too, was later evicted by hospital staffers, and he, too, was rescued by Shuttlesworth.[17]

SEE PAGE 86

A *Birmingham Post-Herald* photographer was clubbed and his camera smashed, but he managed to save his pictures of the Peck beating and get them onto a wire service. Those photographs and others of the burning bus and the beaten riders shocked morning news readers around the world. The press criticized the Klan, the Birmingham police, and the state of Alabama. Birmingham's commissioner of public safety, Theophilus Eugene "Bull" Connor, blamed the absence of police on holiday furlough: it was Mother's Day. Alabama governor John Patterson went on television to say that the riders had brought it on themselves and that he couldn't be expected to protect "a bunch of rabble-rousers." James Farmer ordered a Freedom Ride emblem designed from a combination of the burning-bus image and the Statue of Liberty.

With the riders still besieged and endangered in Birmingham, Attorney General Kennedy negotiated with Shuttlesworth, Patterson, and Connor to guarantee their leaving Alabama alive. Greyhound could not find a driver willing to brave the journey, so the riders were transferred to the airport, where they were again mobbed. With the aid of the Justice Department, the original Freedom Riders eventually flew to New Orleans.

"The students have decided that we can't let violence overcome." Diane Nash was speaking by phone to Shuttlesworth from a student meeting in a Nashville church. "We're going to come to Birmingham to continue the Freedom Ride." "Young lady," Shuttlesworth replied, "do you know that the Freedom Riders were almost killed here?" "Yes," said Nash. "That's exactly why the ride must not be stopped. If they stop us with violence, the movement is dead. We're coming."[18] Nash informed the reverend of the "chickens" that would be coming down, some "speckled," some "Rhode Island Red" (translation: some black riders, some white, in the code used to keep their plans from police wiretappers).

On May 17 the Nashville students boarded a Greyhound bus to Birmingham. Bull Connor protected them from the waiting mob: by locking them up in the bus, then locking them up in jail, then escorting them to the Alabama border. But the students returned, and Attorney General Kennedy again pressured Governor Patterson, who gave reluctant assurance of protection by city and state troopers. On May 20 the Nashville riders set off for Montgomery. As they pulled in to the Montgomery depot, they realized that their guards had disappeared. Once again the riders were set upon by a waiting mob. Rider Jim Zwerg was beaten unconscious, as was the Justice Department's John Siegenthaler.

Robert Kennedy ordered in six hundred federal marshals—the first such intervention by the Kennedy administration (preceding the University of Mississippi incident by sixteen months). Marshals were dispatched to guard the Freedom Riders in hospitals and elsewhere. Twenty-seven Freedom Riders were accompanied by Alabama state troopers and members of the press as their Greyhound bus pulled out of Montgomery on May 24. At the Mississippi border, Mississippi state troopers took over. Farmer, now a rider himself, recalled their elation at the border of the Magnolia State, how one rider burst out singing, "Hallelujah, I'm a travelin'. Hallelujah, ain't it fine. Hallelujah, I'm a travelin' down Freedom's main line."[19]

In Jackson station there was no mob. Instead, police escorted the riders out of the bus, into the white section, out the back, and into police vans. They were arrested, convicted, and sent to jail. Robert Kennedy had worked out a deal with Mississippi Senator James Eastland: no public violence, no federal forces, no desegregation. The Kennedys pressed civil rights leaders for a cooling-off period. Farmer retorted that blacks "have been cooling off for 350 years. If we cool off any more we will be in a deep freeze." Ralph Abernathy was asked by a reporter how he could embarrass the president on the eve of his Vienna summit conference with Nikita Khrushchev. Abernathy answered coolly, through the frame of his mob-shattered car window, "Man, we've been embarrassed all our lives."[20]

That summer, over three hundred Freedom Riders were arrested in Mississippi, where state officials challenged the Supreme Court's ruling on interstate travel. Jail sentences for violating Mississippi segregation laws were long and abusive, and often included such tortures as beating, electric shocks from cattle prods, food deprivation, overheating by day and freezing by night, and solitary confinement. Singers of freedom songs were singled out for extra maltreatment. The punishment and the solidarity that many Freedom Riders experienced in Mississippi penitentiaries deepened their commitment. Some went on to become full-time SNCC workers.

The Freedom Rides and related protests of the summer and fall of 1961 achieved their goals. That September the Interstate Commerce Commission issued regulations that effectively desegregated interstate travel facilities throughout the nation.

PICKETING THE COURTHOUSE, MONROE, NORTH CAROLINA, AUGUST 26, 1961.
DECLAN HAUN

Robert F. Williams, who was an early proponent of armed self-defense in the civil rights movement, headed the NAACP chapter in Monroe. In response to integration protests organized by Williams at the swimming pool and other sites, the Monroe City Council passed an ordinance limiting picketers to ten at a time, marching in single file fifteen feet apart, carrying signs no bigger than twenty-four inches across and containing no inflammatory language. The young woman in this picture, marching on an integrated picket line, was complying with the ordinance.

According to picketer James Forman, the march was met with shouts of "Niggers go home!" "We're going to get Robert Williams!" "Bet she sleeps with a nigger" (referring to a white marcher). The picketers were attacked, and three were arrested. Forman harangued the police, trying to get charges dropped against the arrested marchers and filed against their attackers. "He was the one who started it. Why are you letting him go? There is no justice in Monroe!"

ABOVE: SIT-IN, RALEIGH, NORTH CAROLINA, FEBRUARY 10, 1960. **UNITED PRESS INTERNATIONAL**

OPPOSITE: SIT-IN TRAINING SESSION, VIRGINIA STATE COLLEGE, PETERSBURG, 1960. **EVE ARNOLD**

The massive sit-ins of 1960 were the first major direct action in the civil rights movement since the Montgomery bus boycott. Nineteen sixty was also "freedom year" in Africa, where seventeen new independent nations were established. Rev. James Lawson pointed to Africa to spur on the Nashville sit-ins: "All of Africa will be free before we attain first-class citizenship." James Baldwin commented more sardonically, "All of Africa will be free before we can get a lousy cup of coffee."

A sit-in protester-in-training is subjected to mock harassment. On the left is Dorothy Cotton, who was Rev. Wyatt T. Walker's assistant at the Petersburg Improvement Association and who joined the SCLC staff when Walker was made executive director in the summer of 1960. Cotton became an important member of the SCLC inner circle.

OPPOSITE: ARREST OF A PROTESTER IN DOWNTOWN ATLANTA, WINTER 1963–64. **DANNY LYON**

"One of high school student Taylor Washington's numerous arrests is immortalized as he yells while passing before me. The photograph became the cover of SNCC's photo book, *The Movement*, and was reproduced in the former Soviet Union in *Pravda*, captioned 'Police Brutality USA.'" (Lyon's caption.)

When Danny Lyon met SNCC's executive secretary, James Forman, at the height of the Albany Movement, in August 1962, Forman immediately put the twenty-year-old photographer to work. "'You got a camera?'" Lyon recalls Forman asking. "'Go inside the courthouse. Down the back they have a big water-cooler for whites and next to it a little bowl for Negroes. Go in there and take a picture of that. . . .' My photographs—made because I had studied history, made because I loved to make them, made under the direction of Forman and the [SNCC] office—were used to help create a public image for SNCC. . . . They traveled all across America and even around the world."

ABOVE: SIT-IN BY SNCC STAFF, TODDLE HOUSE, ATLANTA, DECEMBER 1963. **DANNY LYON**

"A Toddle House in Atlanta has the distinction of being occupied during a sit-in by some of the most effective organizers in America when the SNCC staff and supporters take a break from a conference to demonstrate." (Lyon's caption.)

At the counter are (from far left): unidentified woman, Taylor Washington, Joyce Ladner (hand on head), Judy Richardson (looking at camera), unidentified, and Chico Neblett. Standing behind them is Ivanhoe Donaldson. SNCC used another tactic against the Toddle House chain: they bought stock in its parent corporation so they could demonstrate at a board meeting. But, before the meeting, Toddle House capitulated and started to serve black customers.

BELOW: SAM BLOCK OF SNCC BEING LED AWAY FROM
A TIC TOC RESTAURANT, NASHVILLE, NOVEMBER 1962.
HE HAD BEEN STABBED IN THE CHEST WITH A PEN
WHEN HE TRIED TO ENTER. **DANNY LYON**

OPPOSITE: VIGILANTES ATTACKING DOWNTOWN
SHOPPERS, DEXTER AVENUE, MONTGOMERY,
FEBRUARY 27, 1960. **CHARLES MOORE**

By Friday, February 26, sit-ins had spread to Montgomery, and a group of black students tried to get service in the cafeteria at the state capitol building. The next day bands of armed white vigilantes prowled the downtown shopping district. Charles Moore and fellow journalist Ray Jenkins were at the *Montgomery Advertiser*'s offices when they heard about a scuffle in progress. They ran three blocks to catch this attack on female shoppers. Moore's photograph ran on the front page of Sunday's *Advertiser* with a story reporting the name of one of the attackers and indicating that the police had idly stood by; Moore claimed that the crack of bat on head could be heard all the way down the block.

ARRAIGNMENT OF SIT-IN DEMONSTRATORS, MEMPHIS,
1960 OR 1961. **ERNEST WITHERS**

The attorney with his hand on the ledge is Benjamin Hooks
(later national chair of the NAACP).

Presiding judge Beverly Boucher granted the photographer access because he was a former policeman. Withers
was one of the first black officers in Memphis, hired in
1948. He became the outstanding photographer of the
Memphis black community and traveled throughout the
South covering the movement.

DEMONSTRATION, CAIRO, ILLINOIS, AUGUST 1962.
DANNY LYON

John Lewis—Freedom Rider, chairman of SNCC, and now U.S. congressman from Atlanta—kneels at left. "At Cairo's only, and segregated, swimming pool, the group stopped to pray. Then they stood in the street singing, and when a blue pick-up truck drove down the center of the street straight at them, a game of chicken ensued as the truck slowed and the demonstrators moved out of the way, except for one defiant thirteen-year-old girl, who stood her ground until the truck knocked her down."

A variant of this picture was made into a SNCC poster emblazoned "COME LET US BUILD A NEW WORLD TO-GETHER." Ten thousand copies were printed; they sold for a dollar each.

RIGHT: FREEDOM RIDER JIM ZWERG HOSPITALIZED
AFTER HIS BEATING IN THE MONTGOMERY GREYHOUND
STATION, MAY 21, 1961. **JOE HOLLOWAY, JR.**

Zwerg clutches a shot of his own bloodied self on the front
page of the *Montgomery Advertiser*.

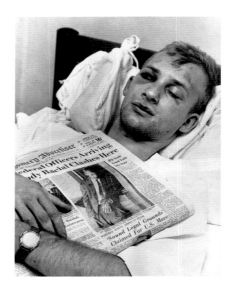

BELOW: FIREBOMBED FREEDOM RIDERS' BUS OUTSIDE
ANNISTON, ALABAMA, MAY 14, 1961. **JOE POSTIGLIONE**

"Passengers of a Greyhound bus, some of them members
of the 'Freedom Riders' group sponsored by the Congress
of Racial Equality (CORE), sit on ground outside burning
bus after it was set afire by group of whites who met the
Negro-white group on arrival here 5/14. After setting bus
afire, whites attacked passengers as they left it. Twelve
persons were treated at an Anniston hospital." (Original
UPI caption.)

FREEDOM RIDE BUS WITH NATIONAL GUARD ESCORT,
MONTGOMERY TO JACKSON, MAY 24–26, 1961.
BRUCE DAVIDSON

4

THE BIRMINGHAM MOVEMENT, 1963
"I Don't Mind Being Bitten by a Dog"

Bull Connor was Birmingham's commissioner of public safety during the 1961 Mother's Day attack on the Freedom Riders. Not all of Birmingham's powerful were happy that Connor let the Klan execute its assault that day. At least, they were not happy with the public relations fallout. The incoming president of the Birmingham Chamber of Commerce was in Tokyo for a business convention when pictures of the bloody ambush appeared in newspapers there. Birmingham suddenly became a lot less attractive to his fellow conventioneers. Something would have to be done about Bull Connor, he remarked.[1]

But in 1963 Connor was still presiding over the most segregated city in the South, "the last stop before Johannesburg, South Africa."[2] Lunch counters and bus terminals, even elevators, were still segregated. The city closed its parks, playgrounds, swimming pools, and golf courses rather than comply with a federal court order to desegregate them. With a population of 350,000, Birmingham was Alabama's largest city. It was a boomtown, built on the steel industry; but the 40 percent of workers who were black were mostly kept out of decent jobs. Birmingham was also a bomb town, called "Bombingham" because of the many dynamite attacks on black houses, churches, and businesses by segregationists—none of them brought to justice.

In 1963 the SCLC applied a radical new strategy to Birmingham: it would organize a citywide protest that would both break local segregation laws and stimulate a national reawakening of conscience. In Fred Shuttlesworth's words: "We wanted confrontation, nonviolent confrontation, to see if it would work on a massive scale. Not just for Birmingham—for the nation. We were trying to launch a systematic, wholehearted battle against segregation which would set the pace for the nation."[3]

Before Birmingham came Albany. In October 1961 Charles Sherrod, an early SNCC "field secretary," was posted, with Cordell Reagon, to Albany, Georgia, a small farming city with a 40 percent black population. First the students, then the entire black community joined together to protest. An "organization of organizations" was formed, called the Albany Movement. Its explicit program was a radical one: to keep up the pressure until all forms of racial discrimination in Albany were dismantled.

To thwart this new movement the Albany police chief, Laurie Pritchett, devised new responses. He decided not to outmuscle but to outsmart his foes. Having studied Martin Luther King, Jr.'s *Stride toward Freedom,* which explained the Gandhian methods behind the Montgomery movement, Pritchett chose to minimize confrontations. He made countless arrests—more than ever before in any one locale—but never on segregation charges. He defeated the jail–no bail strategy by spreading the arrestees among the neighboring county lockups. He worked on splitting the contentious Albany Movement along its various seams of age, occupation, and organizational affiliation.

The Albany Movement eventually enlisted King's help, and his arrival with an entourage of ministers rallied the protesters' energies. But the local SNCC contingent was not pleased, fearing that the community-based leadership they had been nurturing would be deprived of the self-sufficiency it needed to grow. They felt that SNCC had plowed the stony ground, but the SCLC would now harvest the crop—too soon. The elder statesmen (King was all of thirty-three) kept the "hotheads" out of press conferences. "I don't think anybody appreciates going to jail, getting their balls busted day in and day out, and then you don't even get to speak on it. I'm sure we resented all that," Cordell Reagon recalled.[4] Tensions between the major southern civil rights organizations were beginning to surface. SNCC activists were calling King "de Lawd."

King got himself arrested in Albany, hoping to serve the cause by serving time.

PREVIOUS PAGE: WILLIAM GADSDEN ATTACKED BY K-9 UNITS OUTSIDE SIXTEENTH STREET BAPTIST CHURCH, BIRMINGHAM, MAY 3, 1963. **BILL HUDSON**

On May 2, "D Day" of Project C, hundreds of young demonstrators marched out of the Sixteenth Street Baptist Church to their arrest. The next morning Martin Luther King, Jr., announced that even bigger demonstrations would be held that afternoon. Commissioner of Public Safety Bull Connor ordered in police-dog units and water cannons to rout demonstrators from streets around the church and from adjacent Kelly Ingram Park.

This picture had an impact on federal legislation and international relations. Congressman Peter Rodino told a July 1963 House judiciary subcommittee hearing on the Kennedy civil rights bill: "I was attending a conference at Geneva . . . and the incident of the police dog attacking the Negro in Birmingham was printed all over the world. One of the delegates from one of the nations represented at the conference there showed me the front page of the European edition of the Times and he was a little more frank then some of the others, and he asked me, 'Is this the way you practice democracy?' And I had no answer."

But Chief Pritchett had King's bail paid anonymously; King called it a "cunning tactic."[5] After a police officer beat activist Marian King, wife of Albany leader Slater King, into unconsciousness and a miscarriage (in the presence of her three children), the community marched in protest. Police were pelted with stones. "Did you see the nonviolent rocks?" Pritchett asked reporters.[6] Shaken by this breach of discipline, King organized a "Day of Penance."

The Albany Movement was an impassioned failure. Yet the fact remained that fervent protest had been sustained in a small community for over a year (with the help of what would become the most popular and well-traveled civil rights musicians, the Albany Freedom Singers). But little headway was made toward tangibly improving the situation of Albany's blacks. In the end, Pritchett could rightly say, "Albany is as segregated as ever." For King, the lesson was that he should no longer be stepping in and out of crisis situations. "I don't want to be a fireman anymore."[7]

Instead, King would build his own fire. It would burn in Bull Connor's Birmingham and be called "Project C"—C for Confrontation. Project C was initiated at a secretive three-day SCLC retreat in January 1963 that included only a trusted inner circle of eleven leaders. Revs. Shuttlesworth, Wyatt T. Walker, Ralph Abernathy, and King were chosen to lead the operation. King immediately set off on a sixteen-city fund-raising tour and enlisted activist-entertainer Harry Belafonte to raise more money. Great sums were being stockpiled for anticipated bailouts. SCLC executive director Walker and Rev. Shuttlesworth returned to Birmingham to measure march routes, to add up the dollars spent by black shoppers in white stores, and to count lunch counter stools and the students who could fill them. As soon as rumors of these preparations started to spread, the city's business elite was anxious to negotiate. Not since the 1941 March on Washington Movement to integrate defense production had the mere threat of a large protest made such headway.

Birmingham was chosen not just because "the city had been the country's chief symbol of racial intolerance," as King put it,[8] and not just because of Bull Connor's predictable viciousness. It was chosen because of the strength of the SCLC affiliate organization that Shuttlesworth had bolted together over the years. The SCLC would be ferrying a large community on an uncharted voyage, and there was no stauncher vessel than Shuttlesworth's. On top of his organizational skills, Shuttlesworth also had a hell of a preaching style, well suited to firing up emotions.

The Birmingham movement was sustained by an unprecedented run of sixty-five consecutive nightly mass meetings, none of them dull. The sixty-strong Birmingham Movement Choir was famous for its thunderous "Ninety-nine and a Half Won't Do," a song about total commitment to the movement. Bernice Johnson Reagon, one of the Albany Freedom Singers (later founder of the group Sweet Honey in the Rock and a musicologist at the Smithsonian Institution), wrote, "The music of the Birmingham movement reflected its top-drawer level of organization and strategy."[9]

In 1963 the large resources and manpower of the SCLC—a million dollar budget and over one hundred full-time personnel—were concentrated on Birmingham. The SCLC had a leadership and staff whose quality Wyatt Walker liked to compare to that of General Motors. James Lawson headed nonviolence training; by March over two hundred volunteers had signed nonviolence pledge cards and were prepared to brave up to ten days in jail. Diane Nash and her husband, Rev. James Bevel, were hired to organize the student contingents. Two brilliant SCLC directors, Dorothy Cotton and Andrew Young, were brought into town. Dr. King held meeting after meeting, brandished his oratory, played on his international stature, and fine-tuned his cajolery to draw scores of prickly black ministers and civic leaders, each one a potential spoiler, into the fold.

Project C was complex and risky, requiring the skillful manipulation of many elements of Birmingham society. Birmingham's business elite and the northern corporations that owned most of its steel industries would be pressured by boycotts and embarrassed by adverse publicity; the movement's aim was to have them break ranks with the municipal leaders and police. Bull Connor would be provoked into unleashing his arsenal of repression, but the timing of the provocations would have to be just right. And once he responded, the specially constructed high-pressure water cannons, the trained attack dogs, the antiriot tank (army surplus) would have to be endured. Black youth would play a major role; as marchers they would be endangered and would have to be protected. The black community would have to be extraordinarily unified and would have to practice enormous self-control to remain nonviolent.

SEE PAGE 110

Birmingham's black men were not all inclined to nonviolence. Disarming them of their weapons and their desire for vengeance was an early priority. Andrew Marrisett, an SCLC organizer, has recalled: "Every time we saw a guy that was really, really enraged and we thought we could at least talk to right then, we would try to get him to the mass meeting and get him involved. We would sit beside him or close around him, a group of us, and get him involved in the spirit, and we would sing the songs, and do the chants and freedom-now things, and then we'd hear Dr. King speak, and that would quiet down the angriest lion, because he just had that thing about him, that halo that he would shine."[10]

The inauguration of Project C was originally planned to coincide with the Easter shopping season so that the retail boycott would have maximum effect. But the starting date was postponed to await the outcome of municipal elections. Those elections would give Birmingham its first mayor; the old system led by a three-man city commission was being scrapped—largely to get rid of Bull Connor. In the end Connor ran for mayor against a less-flagrant segregationist, Albert Boutwell. Connor lost the vote but refused to step down as commissioner of public safety. So, during the upcoming months Birmingham had two feuding city governments, with Connor still controlling the police and the fire department. With a direct line to Alabama's segregationist governor, George Wallace, Connor also had the power to call in state troops at will.

Project C was designed to proceed dramatically, scene after scene, act following act, building in intensity. As James Bevel put it, "Every nonviolent movement is a dialogue between two forces, and you have to develop a drama to . . . reveal the contradictions in the guys you're dialoguing with within the social context. That's called a socio-drama."[11]

In Phase I the economic boycott would begin, accompanied by small sit-ins and pickets. Phase II called for mass marches on city hall. Phase III would explode on "D Day," with waves of young marchers defying injunctions and filling the jails. Every stage would be accompanied by negotiations with white leaders. Throughout the civil rights era, nonviolent direct action was always accompanied by this expressed readiness to sit down and negotiate.

The campaign finally began on "B Day" (for Birmingham)—April 3, 1963. It was the day after Boutwell's election and Connor's refusal to resign. "A New Day Dawns for Birmingham," proclaimed one newspaper headline. There was a faction that wanted to give the new mayor a chance, but the Project C commanders opted against another delay. A "Birmingham Manifesto" was released to reporters, who mostly ignored it. At the first sit-ins the demonstrators were also ignored by carefully coached waitresses. Twenty-one demonstrators were finally arrested. Mass meetings and handbills publicized the boycott, but local and national newspapers questioned the discrepancy between the campaign's blaring rhetoric and its meager actions. They expressed skepticism about King's leadership ability, which was still under the cloud of the Albany Movement's defeat. Robert Kennedy called the demonstrations "ill-timed." Phase I was not opening to good reviews.

When Phase II began on April 6, things began to get more interesting. A stream of marchers poured out of the Sixteenth Street Baptist Church toward city hall, the first of wave after wave that would roll for thirty-four continuous days. There were forty-five arrests that Saturday, and heated skirmishes and arrests on the next day, Palm Sunday. Large numbers of volunteers began showing up for training and the walk to jail. Nineteen-year-old Leroy Allen was mauled by two police dogs, shocking a large crowd of onlookers. The jails were beginning to fill, and the boycott was gathering momentum. But press coverage was still meager, Birmingham's black businessmen were still opposing the disruptions, and the black community was still too passive.

A breakthrough came on Thursday, April 11. Connor had obtained an injunction against King and the marches—a state injunction, much easier to disobey than the feared federal one, which would have put the movement in the conflicted position of fighting Washington, their sometime ally. King called a news conference to proclaim, "Regardless of what's in this injunction, we've got an injunction from heaven."[12] At a second press conference he announced that he would walk to jail the following day, Good Friday, the anniversary of Jesus' walk to the cross. King's symbolic Good Friday arrest had been planned as a pivotal moment in the Project C script.

Friday morning was heavy with doubt. Bail funds were exhausted. Flouting the

SEE PAGE 101

SEE PAGE 102

injunction might mean long jail terms for King and his followers. It might also prolong the stays of those already jailed, for with the main fund-raiser in jail, who would raise bail? Advice ran for and against King's going through with the arrest. "If we obey this injunction, we are out of business," King decided. He and Abernathy donned stiff new jeans, covered their white collars with blue work shirts, and led fifty marchers to the police vans, escorted by a large crowd of supporters, reporters, and cameramen.

Thrown into solitary confinement, denied even a phone call, King wrote in the margins of newspaper columns the beginning of one of his most important texts, "Letter from Birmingham Jail." The manuscript was smuggled out bit by bit, typescripts and writing paper were smuggled back in. The "Letter" was a deeply felt and lucidly argued apologia, aimed at liberal consciences, for the Birmingham movement and for direct action in general. Widely distributed even before King's release, it remains to this day the most cogent summation of the goals and strategies of the civil rights movement.

King and Abernathy were released on bond after eight days. They were informed about clandestine negotiations with local white business leaders who were looking for a settlement behind Bull Connor's back. As those discussions inched forward, James Bevel was training a huge army of children to spearhead Phase III of Project C. Over and over he projected a copy of an NBC Huntley-Brinkley special report on the 1960 Nashville movement, using film of that earlier youth movement to instruct and inspire the Birmingham kids. Like all Project C tactics, the children's march to jail would combine moral, political, and economic persuasion. Bevel explained: "Most adults have bills to pay—house notes, rents, car notes, utility bills—but the young people . . . are not hooked with all those responsibilities. A boy from high school has the same effect in terms of being in jail, in terms of putting pressure on the city, as his father, and yet there's no economic threat to the family, because the father is still on the job."[13]

Boys and girls went to jail by the hundreds. At one boisterous mass meeting, King urged some third- and fourth-grade volunteers to sit down, but they wouldn't be kept from the front lines. Parents were scared. Censure against exploiting children rained down from white folk in Washington, in the Birmingham establishment, and in the press. King deplored their hypocrisy: "Where had these writers been, we wondered, during the centuries when our segregated social system had been misusing and abusing Negro children? Where had they been with their protective words when, down through the years, Negro infants were born into ghettos, taking their first breath of life in a social atmosphere where the fresh air of freedom was crowded out by the stench of discrimination?" King cited another "answer to the misguided sympathies," the story of an eight-year-old demonstrator questioned by a policeman. "'What do you want' he asked. The child looked into his eyes, unafraid, and gave her answer. 'F'eedom,' she said."[14]

"D Day" was scheduled for Thursday, May 2. Recruiters and leafleteers had put out the word in black high schools, and deejay "Tall Paul" announced a "big party" at

Kelly Ingram Park, across the street from movement headquarters in the Sixteenth Street Baptist Church. Hundreds of trained marchers gathered in the church that morning; outside were hundreds of untrained black supporters and a reinforced detachment of police.

At one o'clock a double file of fifty teenagers issued from the church, singing "We Shall Overcome" in march time. They were shuttled past the police barriers into waiting police vans. A second troop filed down the steps, ready for jail, then a third and a fourth, all children. When the vans could not keep up, patrol cars were jammed with prisoners, then school buses. One troop of students made it past the blockade. They carried their picket signs into white downtown, where Connor's harried forces finally caught them. By four o'clock, 959 children had been sent to jail. In terms of the Gandhian imperative to "fill the jails," it was a glorious day.

On D Day plus one, the forces massed again, including over a thousand children who stayed out of school. Connor was not going to let them get downtown again, even if his jails were packed to their limit. So he prepared a cordon of police dogs and firemen armed with water hoses to contain the protests. Drenched by the hoses, most of the children broke ranks. But one group sat down, refusing to flee. Connor ordered his men to fire on them with "monitor-gun" nozzles that shot streams of water so powerful they could tear bark from trees at one hundred feet or break bones at close range. The jets rolled bodies down the street.

Meanwhile, eight K-9 units were terrorizing prospective marchers at the entrance to Sixteenth Street Baptist. Demonstrators and onlookers alike were set upon by the German shepherds; three teenagers were hospitalized with fang bites. Photographer Bill Hudson captured the nightmarish attack on young Walter Gadsden. A tight-jawed officer in dark aviator glasses is shown pulling the youth into the jaws of the leaping dog. The boy grips the policeman's wrist and looks down at the beast stoicly. He seems to embody "passive resistance."

That photograph and others like it were published around the world. The shot of Gadsden being mauled accompanied headlines the next day in the *New York Times, Washington Post,* and many other papers. The *Post* later printed a letter from a Maryland woman:

> Now I've seen everything. The news photographer who took that picture of a police dog lunging at a human being has shown us in unmistakable terms how low we have sunk and will surely have awakened a feeling of shame in all who have seen that picture, who have any notion of human dignity.
>
> The man being lunged at was not a criminal being tracked down to prevent his murdering other men; he was, and is, a man. If he can have a beast deliberately urged to lunge at him, then so can any man, woman, or child in the United States. . . .
>
> If the United States doesn't stand for some average decent level of human dignity, what does it stand for?[15]

SEE PAGE 103

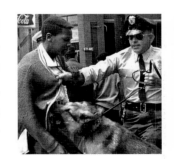

SEE PAGE 89

SEE PAGE 106

SEE PAGE 109

The photographs of the Birmingham movement remain the most gripping of all civil rights photography. Without them Project C might have been just another guttering local struggle, another Albany. Instead, it became a movement that persuaded the world. The photos of the dogs and the hoses were conjured up in countless speeches and writings as the epitome of American racial brutality.[16] The repercussions were international. The *Post* ran a story about how the Birmingham struggles were "front page news in Europe," giving people there the impression "that the United States is a land of brutality and repression."[17] Malcolm X asked an African audience at the University of Ghana, "How can you [the African nations in the United Nations] condemn Portugal and South Africa while our Black people are being bitten by dogs and beaten with clubs?"[18]

Birmingham stayed on the front pages of the *Times* and the *Post* for twelve days. The stories and images of Bull Connor's barbarities brought sympathy and support (including money) to the Birmingham movement from many. But others saw the victims in these pictures as cynical inciters of justified riot-control measures. An extraordinary lead article in *Life* magazine's May 17 issue covered the Birmingham demonstrations. Featuring eleven pages of Charles Moore's powerful photographs, the story is titled "They Fight a Fire That Won't Go Out." The article pays lip service to the ideal of equal rights, but its main point is that the violence had been provoked by black movement leaders. The word *nonviolence* is always in skeptical quotes. "Simmering racial hatred" is attributed to blacks. Not a single black voice is quoted. Instead, the article concludes with a page of sixteen quotes from "a cross section of Birmingham's white residents," all of them critical of the demonstrations.

So, press coverage of the Birmingham protests was mixed, sympathetic only to the degree that the protesters were considered innocent victims. Political support followed the same pattern. Members of the U.S. House and Senate rose to speak about Birmingham, but only about half supported the demonstrations.

In addition to eliciting reactions across the nation and beyond, news of the May attacks also opened a new act in the Birmingham drama. The previously fractious black community was enraged by Bull Connor's assaults and enlarged its support for the protests. The white power structure became defensive. White businessmen distanced themselves from both Connor and King. The Justice Department flew in an emissary to facilitate discussions between moderates on both sides. Demonstrations, arrests, and jailings; dog attacks, hosings, and clubbings went on for days. Reactive violence by blacks was increasing; rocks were thrown, and more and more guns were carried. Movement leaders feared losing control, feared being set back by riots. They stepped up nonviolence training.

At the same time, there were premonitions of victory. At one mass meeting a jovial King told a joke about the redundancy of dousing Baptists. "And dogs?" he said. "Well, I'll tell you. When I was growing up, I was dog bitten—for NOTHING! So I don't mind being bitten by a dog for standing up for freedom!"[19]

Monday, May 6, was the biggest day yet for arrests. Comedian Dick Gregory led a troop to jail. Parents were seen walking with their children into bondage. Four churches were needed to hold that night's mass meeting. One of King's orations that evening was recorded:

> Never in the history of this nation have so many people been arrested for the cause of freedom and dignity. You know, there are approximately 2500 people in jail right now. . . . As long as we keep moving like we're moving, the power structure of Birmingham will have to give in. And we're probably nearer to a solution of this problem than we're able to realize. And don't you worry about your children. They are gonna be all right. Don't hold them back if they want to go to jail. For they are doing a job for not only themselves, but for all of America and all of mankind. Somewhere we read, "A little child shall lead them."[20]

The last line was greeted with peals of assent.

Within the movement there was hot debate about the uses and abuses of young hostages. Many of the arrested children were being held outdoors, even on cold, rainy nights. When SNCC's James Forman became aware of the conditions, he took King to visit one compound. They saw friends and relatives throw blankets and food over the fence to the shivering, hungry young prisoners. But King decided not to hold back the youth brigades.

On May 7 "Operation Confusion" was put into effect. A daring and complicated operation full of subterfuges and decoys, it landed thousands of picketers in Birmingham's white downtown. The police were overwhelmed; arrests could not be made because the jails were already bursting. Duels with water cannons and rocks erupted. When Fred Shuttlesworth was hospitalized after being pounded against the wall of Sixteenth Street Baptist with a monitor-gun water hose, Bull Connor commented, "I wish they had carried him away in a hearse."[21] An emergency session of the Senior Citizens Committee brought seventy of the "big mules" of the white business establishment to the downtown Chamber of Commerce office. With sirens and picketers' chants in their ears, they debated how to end the conflict speedily, either through a negotiated settlement or by calling in Governor Wallace's troops—or even those of President Kennedy.

"The City of Birmingham has reached an accord with its conscience."[22] Fred Shuttlesworth made this announcement on May 10 at a news conference attended by over 150 reporters from around the world. An accord had finally been pounded into shape by the SCLC and the white business leaders. In exchange for an end to demonstrations the compromise guaranteed the desegregation of retail facilities and the nondiscriminatory hiring and promoting of black industrial workers. Not all whites supported the settlement. Connor and his co-commissioners called it a "capitulation by certain weak-kneed white people under threat of violence by the rabble-rousing Negro, King." The Ku Klux Klan staged a rally where Imperial Wizard Robert Shelton predicted, "Martin Luther King's epitaph, in my opinion, can be written here in Birmingham."[23]

The night of Shelton's speech, King's room at the Gaston Motel was dynamited, as was his brother's house. There were no fatalities, but rioting broke out, with several buildings and cars set afire. The rampage was aggravated by the brutal state troopers sent in by Governor Wallace, whose intention it was to sabotage the desegregation agreement. Only after President Kennedy dispatched federal troops to the city was calm restored. The agreement was eventually implemented for the most part—but not before many more bombings.

One month later Wallace stood on the University of Alabama campus at Tuscaloosa to bar the registration of its first black students. He was forced to step aside by federal troops. That night, June 11, 1963, President Kennedy delivered a speech on national television that Martin Luther King, Jr., called "one of the most eloquent, profound and unequivocal pleas for Justice and the Freedom of all men ever made by any President."[24]

> We preach freedom around the world and we mean it. And we cherish our freedom here at home. But are we to say to the world—and, much more importantly, to each other—that this is the land of the free except for Negroes; that we have no second-class citizens, except Negroes; that we have no class or caste system, no ghettoes, no master race, except with respect to Negroes.
>
> Now the time has come for this nation to fulfill its promise. The events in Birmingham and elsewhere have so increased the cries for equality that no city or state legislative body can prudently ignore them. The fires of frustration and discord are burning in every city, North and South. . . .
>
> We face, therefore, a moral crisis, as a country and a people. It cannot be met by repressive police action. It cannot be left to increased demonstrations in the streets. It cannot be quieted by token moves or talks. It is time to act in the Congress, in your state and local legislative bodies, in all of our daily lives. . . .
>
> Next week I shall ask the Congress of the United States to act, to make a commitment it has not fully made in this century to the proposition that race has no place in American life and law.[25]

Kennedy concluded his speech by outlining a major civil rights bill that he would soon send to Congress.

The day after the speech, on June 12, Medgar Evers, the Mississippi NAACP leader, was dead from a shotgun blast in his back, the first political leader to be assassinated in the civil rights era. Evers was buried in Arlington National Cemetery with full military honors.

SNCC WORKERS VISITING A SUPPORTER, NEAR ALBANY,
GEORGIA, 1963. **DANNY LYON**

Charles Sherrod, who headed SNCC's efforts in southwest
Georgia, is on the right; Randy Battle is seated at center. In
Albany during the summer of 1961 Sherrod and Cordell
Reagon set up the first SNCC field outpost. They spent their
first days on the basketball courts there getting to know people; they ended up sparking one of the most important civil
rights movements.

This photograph captures the fervor of the freedom songs that were so important to the civil rights movement in Georgia and throughout the nation.

As early as 1788 one of the first black congregations in North America, the First African Baptist, was established in Savannah. In 1961 Martin Luther King, Jr., delivered an early version of his "I Have a Dream" speech there.

Photographer Kenneth Thompson traveled widely documenting civil rights events for the National Council of Churches.

RIGHT: MARTIN LUTHER KING, JR., ANNOUNCES AT A PRESS CONFERENCE THAT HE WILL NOT COMPLY WITH AN INJUNCTION AGAINST MARCHING, GASTON MOTEL, BIRMINGHAM, APRIL 11, 1963. **ERNST HAAS**

BELOW: ABERNATHY AND KING WALK TOWARD THEIR
ARREST IN BIRMINGHAM, ON GOOD FRIDAY, APRIL 12,
1963. **CHARLES MOORE**

OPPOSITE, TOP: ARREST OF A DEMONSTRATOR
OUTSIDE THE CARVER THEATRE, BIRMINGHAM,
MAY 1963. **BRUCE DAVIDSON**

OPPOSITE, BOTTOM: YOUNG DEMONSTRATORS
TAUNTING A POLICEMAN, MAY 1963. **CHARLES MOORE**

DEMONSTRATOR ATTACKED BY POLICE DOGS,
MAY 3, 1963. **CHARLES MOORE**

According to SCLC field staffer Tommy Wrenn, the man being mauled in this picture had been recruited from a nearby pool hall to organize his friends and particularly to keep them from responding violently to police violence.

POLICE-DOG ATTACKS AND PHOTOGRAPHERS,
MAY 3, 1963. **BIRMINGHAM NEWS**

This photograph was taken moments after the picture
on page 89—Gadsden's sweater is now torn. In the center, Charles Moore is seen taking a variant of the picture
seen opposite.

LEFT: FIREMEN TRYING TO DISLODGE DEMONSTRATORS WITH HIGH-PRESSURE WATER HOSES, CORNER OF FIFTH AVENUE NORTH AND SEVENTEENTH STREET, MAY 3, 1963. **CHARLES MOORE**

ABOVE: DEMONSTRATORS BLASTED AGAINST A DOORWAY, SEVENTEENTH STREET, MAY 3, 1963. **CHARLES MOORE**

On May 3 Moore broke off from another assignment when radio reports out of Birmingham alerted him to the intensity of the events there. His pictures of the dog and water-cannon attacks were taken as soon as he arrived in town. They were published in the May 17 issue of *Life*, in an eleven-page lead story that ran under Moore's byline. While he was photographing, Moore was hit by a concrete block thrown from a roof, which damaged the tendons in his ankle. Limping painfully, he stayed on the job for several days, until he was arrested on May 7. After jumping bail the next day, he was forbidden to reenter Alabama, where he and his family resided, until the charges were eventually resolved.

DEMONSTRATOR ATTACKED WITH WATER CANNONS,
KELLY INGRAM PARK, MAY 3, 1963. **CHARLES MOORE**

After these pictures were taken, the officer chased this
demonstrator, wrestled her to the ground, and arrested her.

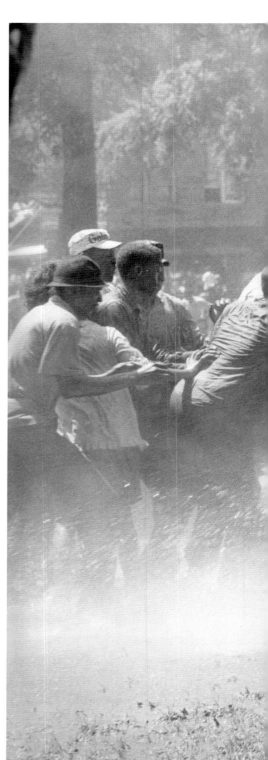

ABOVE AND RIGHT: DEMONSTRATORS ATTACKED WITH
WATER CANNONS, KELLY INGRAM PARK, MAY 3, 1963.
CHARLES MOORE

OPPOSITE: DANELLA BRYANT PRAYING DURING A
DEMONSTRATION OUTSIDE THE TRAFFIC ENGINEERING
BUILDING, BIRMINGHAM, MAY 5, 1963. **GARY HAYNES**

Danella Bryant was a seventeen-year-old Parker High School
senior active in the movement:

> I was really, really involved. And the reason I could
> be involved, unlike some of my peers, was that my father
> owned his own business. He wasn't easily intimidated.
> . . . I didn't realize at the time how dangerous the situa-
> tion was. The only thing I was concerned with was that I
> wanted my freedom, I wanted to be able to go where I
> wanted, like everybody else did. . . . I couldn't understand
> why everybody didn't leave [school to demonstrate]. But
> as I look back now, I realize that they were really afraid.
> Their parents had jobs and they were afraid that they
> would lose their jobs, and they were afraid, especially
> the seniors, that they wouldn't graduate. In fact, I thought
> maybe I wouldn't graduate, but I did. . . . A few teachers
> —I said they were Uncle Toms at the time—they were
> afraid and felt like we shouldn't be doing what we were
> doing, that things would happen in time. And I told them
> that we ought to speed those things up, we got to let the
> whole world know what's happening in Birmingham. . . .
> The world needed to know. The world did know.

RIGHT: MYRLIE EVERS CONSOLING HER SON AT THE
FUNERAL OF MEDGAR EVERS, ARLINGTON NATIONAL
CEMETERY, JUNE 1963. **JOHN LOENGARD**

This picture was on the cover of *Life* magazine. The cover
story, headlined "He Said He Wouldn't Mind Dying If . . . ,"
was written by Myrlie Evers. (Mrs. Evers-Williams is currently chair of the NAACP.) The article concluded: "So I
grieve, but I do not regret. We had a wonderful eleven years
together. Some people are left with nothing: I have magnifi-
cent memories. Medgar didn't belong just to me—he belonged
to so many, many people everywhere. He was so willing to
give his life that I feel his death has served a certain purpose.
When I find myself in pits of depression, I remind myself that
fulfilling this purpose is what he really wanted."

It took over thirty years and several trials to bring to justice the murderer of the first martyred leader of the civil rights
movement. In 1994 Byron de la Beckwith, a notorious white
supremacist from Grenada, Mississippi, was convicted of the
murder of Medgar Evers and sentenced to life imprisonment.

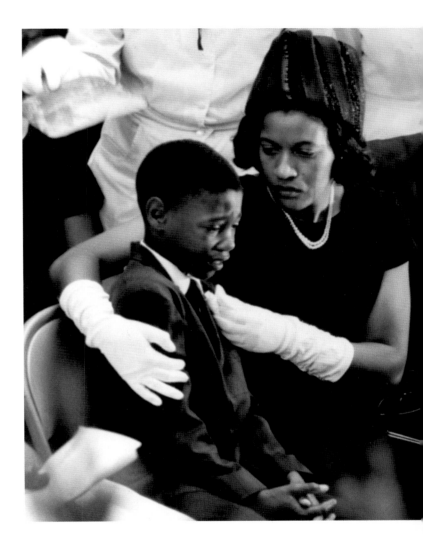

5

THE MARCH ON WASHINGTON, 1963

"We Stood on a Height"

In the spring and summer of 1963 the events in Birmingham inspired a wave of demonstrations elsewhere, more extensive than all that had come before. Almost a thousand actions were mounted in over a hundred southern cities, resulting in over twenty thousand arrests. On June 19 President Kennedy sent Congress the promised civil rights bill, which offered federal protection to African Americans seeking to vote, to shop, to eat out, and to be educated on equal terms. Pressuring Congress to adopt this bill and consolidating the huge upsurge in protest activities brought together major civil rights, labor, and religious groups to organize a massive Washington demonstration.

The roots of the 1963 March on Washington go back to a 1941 initiative by A. Philip Randolph, the trailblazing president of the Brotherhood of Sleeping Car Porters. Randolph had organized the original March on Washington Movement, which was designed to pressure President Roosevelt to guarantee jobs for black men and women in the wartime armament industries. The 1941 march was canceled at the last moment when Roosevelt capitulated to the demands and issued the first executive order protecting African-American rights since the Emancipation Proclamation. After the war Randolph also succeeded in persuading President Harry S. Truman to ban racial discrimination in the military.

At the end of 1962 Randolph began to talk to organizer Bayard Rustin about staging a big Washington demonstration. They conceived of two days of rallying and lobbying "to embody in one gesture civil rights as well as national economic demands." A coalition would be formed to bring in as many people as possible. A massive protest gathering might be accompanied by direct-action campaigns, such as sit-ins in congressional offices.

Martin Luther King, Jr., had also been thinking about some new and larger form

of demonstration. He said to his aides, "We are on a breakthrough. . . . We need a mass protest," and told them that offers of help had come from certain trade unions and from Paul Newman and Marlon Brando—both "Kennedy men."[1] King asked the aides to contact Randolph to see if they could all work together. On June 11—the same day that Kennedy made his historic civil rights speech and the eve of Medgar Evers's murder—King announced to the press plans for a march on Washington.

On July 2, at New York's Roosevelt Hotel, a march organization was established at a meeting attended by the "Big Six" civil rights leaders: Randolph, Roy Wilkins (NAACP), James Farmer (CORE), John Lewis (SNCC), Whitney Young, Jr. (Urban League), and King (SCLC). Bayard Rustin was named chief coordinator of the march, overcoming some skittish opposition based on his being a pacifist, socialist, and homosexual.

Randolph and Rustin originally planned to stress economic inequities and to press for a new federal jobs program and a higher minimum wage. A nationwide recession that had begun in 1959 was still in progress in 1963. The black unemployment rate was twice that of whites, with over one and a half million blacks looking for work. To stress these economic concerns—in addition to the standard civil rights agenda—the massive protest was dubbed the "March on Washington for Jobs and Freedom." But the events in Birmingham and the Kennedy civil rights bill changed the agenda; the emphasis shifted to lobbying for the civil rights bill that was wending its way through Congress.

The march was scheduled for August 28. That left just under two months for Rustin (working out of an office on Harlem's West 130th Street) to organize the turnout and handle the logistics of getting an expected 100,000 demonstrators in and out of town. Within two weeks he had distributed two thousand copies of his *Organizing Manual No. One* to movement leaders at centers throughout the nation.

The budget for the march organization was put at $120,000—a huge sum. Funds came in through big donations and small. Official march buttons were sold for a quarter each, with 175,000 sold by August 17 and 150,000 more on order. The official memento of the march, sold for one dollar, was a portfolio of five red, white, blue, and black collage-based prints that incorporated *Life* magazine photographs of dog and fire-hose attacks and other movement dramas; forty thousand were printed.[2] A big fund-raiser lit up Harlem's Apollo Theatre on the Friday night before the march. William "Cozy" Cole, Herbie Mann, Quincy Jones, Tony Bennett, Thelonious Monk, Carmen McRae, and Billy Eckstine were among those donating performances. Josephine Baker, James Baldwin, and Burt Lancaster led a march in Paris to support the upcoming one in Washington.[3]

President Kennedy tried to persuade the leadership to cancel the march. "We

SEE PAGE 127

want success in Congress, not just a big show at the Capitol. Some of these people are looking for an excuse to be against us; and I don't want to give any of them a chance to say 'Yes, I'm for the bill, but I am damned if I will vote for it at the point of a gun.'"[4] Failing to stop it, Kennedy publicly embraced the march.

Fears of a possible riot were intense, and the Washington authorities and the march organizers were determined to ensure a peaceful day. D.C. police units had all their leaves canceled; neighboring suburban forces were given special riot-control training. With Birmingham in mind, the attorney general expressly forbade the presence of police dogs. Liquor sales were banned for a day—for the first time since Prohibition. Two Washington Senators' baseball games were postponed. The Justice Department and the army coordinated preparations for emergency troop deployments; seventy different potential emergency scenarios were studied. A crew of lawyers was convened to prepare in advance proclamations authorizing military deployments. Fifteen thousand paratroopers were put on alert. The Justice Department and the police worked with the march committee to develop a state-of-the-art public-address system; unbeknownst to the march coordinators, the police rigged the system so that they could take control of it if trouble arose. The main rally would be at the Lincoln Memorial. For the organizers, that site had a powerful symbolism, particularly on the centennial of the Emancipation Proclamation. The police liked the site because, with water on three sides, the demonstrators could be easily contained.

FBI director J. Edgar Hoover repeatedly tried to scuttle the march. In the months leading up to it he intensified his already passionate campaign to defame Martin Luther King, Jr. Hoover tried to persuade the Kennedys that King was being influenced by Communists, and his specious denunciations of some King associates were taken much more seriously by the Kennedys than was warranted. As a result, they strong-armed King into cutting off some of his closest friends and advisers on the grounds that they might be enemy agents. Hoover's baseless suspicions about King, his virulent attacks on him, and his repeated attempts to destroy his reputation with the Kennedys were spurred by racist delusions and other pathological animosities. Hoover tried, unsuccessfully, to exploit wiretap information about King's sexual indiscretions and about Rustin's homosexual liaisons. On the very morning of the march, Hoover assigned several agents to telephone celebrity participants in a futile last-ditch attempt to get them to withdraw their support. His attacks on King are some of the darkest examples of official paranoia and character assassination in America.

For the marchers, the trip to Washington was an often festive affair, enlivened with freedom songs and the excitement of participating in what they knew to be a historic action. Most demonstrators came in buses chartered by local branches of the movement; another thirty thousand or so arrived in twenty-one chartered trains. On August 28, the day of the march, New York's Penn Station reported the largest early morning crowd since the end of World War II. Members of CORE's Brooklyn chapter walked the 230 miles to the march in thirteen days. Three of the first arrivals were Robert Thomas, age eighteen; Robert Avery, seventeen; and James F. Smith, sixteen—all veterans of the Gadsden (Alabama) Student Movement. Arriving almost a week ahead of time after a 700-mile walk and hitchhike, they were housed and put to work by Rev. Walter Fauntroy, head of the Washington branch of the SCLC. Surveys indicate that about 15 percent of the participants were students, about 25 percent were white, and a majority of the black participants were middle class, northern, and urban. Estimates of the crowd size range from 200,000 to 500,000. It was unquestionably the largest political demonstration in the United States to date.

SEE PAGE 124

Demonstrators' signs and slogans ranged from the mass-produced to the unique. The United Auto Workers union, one of the march's biggest sponsors, printed hundreds of signs with slogans such as "UAW Says Jobs and Freedom for Every American." A young black man in a white shirt and tie wrote on his sign "There Would *Be* More of *Us* Here But So Many of Us Are in *Jail*. Freedom *Now*." A young white woman painted "Stop Legal Murders" on her sign. On the day before the march Robert Moses picketed the Justice Department with a sign reading, "When There Is No Justice, What Is the State But a Robber Band Enlarged?" A young black woman in a paisley dress carried a sign reading, "Not 'Negroes' But AfroAmericans! We Must Be Accorded Full Rights as Americans Not in the Future but Now." (Debates over appropriate labels were heating up in the summer of 1963. "Negro" was used almost exclusively in the march speeches; only John Lewis referred to "black people" and "the black masses.") One elderly black man ingeniously covered twenty-one slats of a five-foot-wide venetian blind with his poem "Martyr Medgar Evers," one stanza of which read:

> Ole Glory's tarnished with his blood
> for having shabbily allowed
> a noble son to be downtrod
> because he was both black and proud![5]

The demonstrators gathered at the Washington Monument, where a stage had been set up for morning entertainment. Joan Baez opened the program with "Oh Freedom" and also led a rendition of "We Shall Overcome." Other performers included Odetta; Josh White (Bayard Rustin had been his sideman thirty years earlier); the Albany Freedom Singers; Bob Dylan; and Peter, Paul and Mary, whose version of Dylan's civil rights anthem "Blowin' in the Wind" was then number two on the charts (after Martha and the Vandellas' "Heat Wave").

Before noon and ahead of schedule, impatient demonstrators began to march up Independence and Constitution Avenues to the Lincoln Memorial. The march leaders got word of this surprise development while lobbying on Capitol Hill, and they rushed to join the advancing throng. Enterprising march marshals opened a passageway for them so that they could be photographed arm in arm "leading" the march.

Press coverage was more extensive than for any previous political demonstration in U.S. history. A huge tent near the Lincoln Memorial held the march committee's "News HQ." The committee issued no fewer than 1,655 special press passes, augmenting the 1,220 members of the regular Washington press corps. News agencies sent large crews of reporters and photographers—some assigned to celebrities, others to everyday marchers, others to aerial coverage. Leading newspapers in many countries ran the march story on their front pages. It was also one of the first events to be broadcast live around the world, via the newly launched communications satellite Telstar. The three major television networks spent over three hundred thousand dollars (more than twice the march committee's budget) to broadcast the event. CBS covered the rally "gavel to gavel," from 1:30 to 4:30, canceling *As the World Turns, Password, Art Linkletter's House Party, To Tell the Truth, The Edge of Night,* and *Secret Storm.*

SEE PAGE 122

The huge audience heard many speakers and singers, both scheduled and unscheduled. One of the first, reading a speech written by James Baldwin, was Charlton Heston, representing an "arts contingent" that included Ossie Davis, Marlon Brando, Sammy Davis, Jr., Sidney Poitier, Lena Horne, Diahann Carroll, Paul Newman, and Harry Belafonte. Josephine Baker, wearing her Free French uniform with her Legion of Honor decoration, was the only woman to speak at the rally. The exclusion of women speakers had been debated, with the all-male leadership opting for only a "Tribute to Women": Rustin introduced to the roaring crowd Rosa Parks, Daisy Bates, Diane Nash, Gloria Richardson (a leader from Cambridge, Maryland), and Mrs. Herbert Lee (widow of the slain Mississippi activist), as well as citing Myrlie Evers in absentia. Marian Anderson, the great contralto, made it to the platform too late to lead the national anthem as planned; instead, she later sang "He's Got the Whole World in His Hands."

In his speech NAACP president Roy Wilkins warned President Kennedy not to let his already overmoderate civil rights bill be further watered down. Wilkins also announced the death in Ghana that morning of W.E.B. Du Bois, father of pan-Africanism and of the NAACP.

Whitney Young's speech, which focused on urban inequities, was addressed to future black marchers:

They must march from the rat infested, overcrowded ghettos to decent, wholesome, unrestricted residential areas dispersed throughout the cities. They must march from the relief rolls to the established retraining centers. . . . They must march from the cemeteries where our young, our newborn die three times sooner, and our parents die seven years earlier. . . . They must march from the congested, ill-equipped schools which breed dropouts and which smother motivation. . . . And finally, they must march from a present feeling of despair and hopelessness, despair and frustration, to renewed faith and confidence.[6]

The most controversial speech was given by John Lewis. When a draft of the speech was circulated in advance, march leaders and Attorney General Kennedy raised strenuous objections to Lewis's calling the Kennedy civil rights bill "too little, too late" and especially to his rhetoric: "We will march through the South, through the Heart of Dixie, the way Sherman did. We will pursue our own 'scorched earth' policy and burn Jim Crow to the ground—nonviolently. We will fragment the South into a thousand pieces and put them back together in the image of democracy."[7] A compromise speech was hammered out only after the aging Randolph made a personal appeal to Lewis and other SNCC leaders not to mar the occasion that he had worked for all his life. Lewis's toned-down speech was received with unmatched enthusiasm; it was interrupted by applause fourteen times. When he finished, Lewis walked past the other leaders on the platform. Every black hand reached out for his, while every white speaker sat still, staring into space.

After Lewis, Mahalia Jackson stepped up to warm the crowd in anticipation of the final scheduled speaker, Martin Luther King, Jr. She sang the gospel classic, "I've Been 'Buked and I've Been Scorned." A journalist has eloquently described the response to her performance: "The button-down men in front and the old women in back came to their feet screaming and shouting. They had not known that this thing was in them, and that they wanted it touched. From different places and different ways, with different dreams they had come, and now, hearing this sung, they were one."[8]

At the end of a long procession of speech and song, Martin Luther King, Jr., stepped up to the podium to deliver the closing address. Part of it had been written during the preceding hurried hours, parts of it rehearsed many times. With its final crescendo improvised in response to the crowd, "I Have a Dream" became instantly famous and remains one of the great moments of modern oratory. King began, "I am happy to join with you today in what will go down in history as the greatest demonstration for freedom in the history of our nation." He concluded:

> When we allow freedom to ring, when we let it ring from every village and every hamlet, from every state and every city, we will be able to speed up that day when all God's children, black men and white men, Jews and Gentiles, Protestants and Catholics, will be able to join hands and sing in the words of the old Negro spiritual: "Free at last! Free at last! Thank God Almighty, we are free at last!"[9]

The D.C. police reported that within half an hour after the closing anthem, "We Shall Overcome," only a couple thousand marchers remained in the vicinity of the Lincoln Memorial. As the crowd withdrew, Rustin noticed Randolph standing alone at the dais. He walked over and put his arm around the old man's shoulder and said,

"Mr. Randolph, it looks like your dream has come true." Randolph replied that it was "the most beautiful and glorious day of his life." Rustin saw tears streaming down his friend's face.[10]

As the marchers dispersed, thrilled with new confidence in their strength, the leaders rushed to a White House strategy meeting on the pending civil rights bill. When they entered the Cabinet Room, the president smiled at King and said, "I have a dream," acknowledging a catchy refrain. Kennedy felt that the march had been nice but it would hardly extricate him from the political dilemma posed by the bill. Foreseeing disaster for the Democrats if he backed it too forcefully, he would not give the civil rights leaders a strong commitment of support.

SEE PAGE 126

Some movement stalwarts felt that the march had been manipulated by the president to project a prettified image of racial harmony. Malcolm X called it the "Farce on Washington." Historian Clayborne Carson, who was attending his first civil rights demonstration, originally experienced it as an "epiphany" but then had second thoughts when Stokely Carmichael of SNCC told him it was "only a sanitized, middle-class version of the real black movement."[11]

But the size and diversity of the gathered masses, the pageantry of their display, the emotional intensity of the songs and speeches, and the peacefulness and good humor of everyone under the hot sun deeply impressed most observers. Russell Baker wrote in the *New York Times:* "No one could remember an invading army quite as gentle as the two hundred thousand civil-rights marchers who occupied Washington today. . . . The sweetness and patience of the crowd may have set some sort of national high-water mark in mass decency."[12]

On Sunday, September 15, barely two weeks after the march, Birmingham's Sixteenth Street Baptist Church was celebrating Youth Day. The church was full of children. A bomb was flung from a speeding car. The explosion injured twenty-one children and killed four young girls.

SEE PAGE 128

On November 22 President Kennedy was assassinated in Dallas. On July 2, 1964, the Civil Rights Act of 1964 was passed by Congress. The act banned racial discrimination in public facilities and in voting rights, but it proved to be only one step forward toward a distant goal.

THE MARCH ON WASHINGTON FOR JOBS AND FREEDOM:
THE CROWD GATHERING AT THE WASHINGTON MONUMENT,
AUGUST 28, 1963. **BOB ADELMAN**

The March on Washington for Jobs and Freedom of 1963 was the
largest political demonstration in U.S. history to that date and
still one of the most vividly remembered. James Baldwin wrote,
"That day, for a moment, it almost seemed that we stood on a
height, and could see our inheritance; perhaps we could make
the kingdom real, perhaps the beloved community would not forever remain the dream one dreamed in agony.

BELOW: CONGREGATING AT THE WASHINGTON MONUMENT.
NAT HERZ

Photographer Nat Herz rode to the march in a chartered bus with fellow CORE members. After his return home, he excitedly assembled a book of words and photographs to "give basic justice to this day of history and hope." He wrote: "What was the mood of the standing, sitting, thousands and thousands of waiting people? Well, here we are, well here we are, great God a mighty here we are! It's beautiful! Has anything like this ever been seen? Great God a mighty we are here! Great God a mighty I am here! Great lord a plenty, 20,000 I's are here! Fine to be here, glad to be here, mighty, mighty proud to be here!"

OPPOSITE: SINGING DEMONSTRATORS AT THE
WASHINGTON MONUMENT. LEONARD FREED

ABOVE: THE POST-RALLY MEETING IN THE WHITE
HOUSE CABINET ROOM. **UNITED PRESS INTERNATIONAL**

Left to right: Whitney Young, Jr. (Urban League); Martin
Luther King, Jr. (SCLC); John Lewis (SNCC); Rabbi Joachim
Prinz (American Jewish Congress); Dr. Eugene Carson
Blake (National Council of Churches); A. Philip Randolph;
President Kennedy; Walter Reuther (United Auto Work-
ers); and Vice President Johnson (behind Reuther).

The meeting lasted seventy-two minutes and concentrated on the political maneuvering that would be needed
to get the Kennedy civil rights bill through Congress.

RIGHT: MARTIN LUTHER KING, JR., GIVING THE "I HAVE
A DREAM" SPEECH. **BOB ADELMAN**

To the right of King is Bayard Rustin, the primary organizer
of the march.

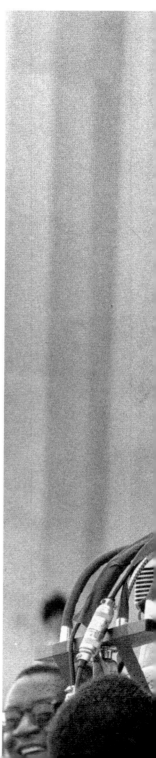

MOURNERS AT THE JOINT FUNERAL OF ADDIE MAE COLLINS, DENISE MCNAIR, AND CYNTHIA WESLEY, SIXTEENTH STREET BAPTIST CHURCH, SEPTEMBER 18, 1963. **DANNY LYON**

Four girls perished in the September 5 bombing of Youth Day classes: Addie Mae Collins, age fourteen; Carol Robertson, fourteen; Cynthia Wesley, fourteen; and Denise McNair, eleven.

As historian Taylor Branch relates: "[Maxine] McNair searched desperately for her only child until she finally came upon a sobbing old man and screamed, 'Daddy, I can't find Denise!' The man helplessly replied, 'She's dead, baby. I've got one of her shoes.' He held a girl's white dress shoe, and the look on his daughter's face made him scream out, 'I'd like to blow the whole town up!'"

Fourteen years later, Robert Chambliss was convicted of the murder of Denise McNair and sentenced to life in prison, where he died in 1985. Chambliss was a Klansman who proudly bore the nickname "Dynamite Bob."

REV. FRED SHUTTLESWORTH ADDRESSING THE JOINT
FUNERAL. **DANNY LYON**

GLORIA RICHARDSON FACING OFF NATIONAL GUARDSMEN,
CAMBRIDGE, MARYLAND, MAY 1964. **FRED WARD**

In 1962–64 Gloria Richardson led the black community in an extensive series of demonstrations against and negotiations with the white power structure of Cambridge, Maryland —the seat of Dorchester County, on the Chesapeake Bay, not far from Washington, D.C. The National Guard occupied Cambridge from June 14, 1963, through July 7, 1964.

According to historian Annette Brock: "In some ways, Cambridge was unique. It was the first grass-roots movement outside the deep South; it was one of the first campaigns to focus on economic conditions rather than just civil rights, the Kennedy administration intervened on a broader scale than ever before (the actual signing of an 'Accord' took place); nonviolence was questioned as a tactic; and it was the first major movement of which a woman was the leader."

SNCC PHOTOGRAPHER CLIFFORD VAUGHS IS ARRESTED
BY THE NATIONAL GUARD, CAMBRIDGE, MARYLAND,
MAY 2, 1964. DANNY LYON

"That night Clifford Vaughs, who was from California and had recently begun to make pictures for SNCC, handed me his flash, saying he didn't need it because he was going to be arrested. People were sitting down in the street. Someone hurled a bottle towards the guard troops, and Gloria Richardson mounted a National Guard jeep to ask for calm. Then the guard tried to arrest Clifford, and a tug-of-war developed as demonstrators held Clifford's feet while the guard pulled him away."

6

SNCC AND MISSISSIPPI, 1960–64

"A Tremor in the Middle of the Iceberg"

In the summer of 1960 Robert Moses, a twenty-five-year-old Harlem native with a graduate degree in philosophy from Harvard, was stuffing envelopes in the tiny Atlanta office shared by the SCLC and SNCC. SNCC and the sit-in movement were just months old. SNCC's single staffer, poet Jane Stembridge, suggested that Moses help recruit black leaders from the Deep South for an upcoming conference. Ella Baker sent Moses to meet one of the bravest leaders, Amzie Moore, in Cleveland, Mississippi. Cleveland was about thirty-five miles from Indianola, where leading segregationist Senator James Eastland had his plantation and where the First White Citizens Council had been born in 1954. Cleveland was also near Money, where (five years before Moses' arrival), Emmett Till had been beaten, shot, and thrown into the Tallahatchie River.

These places were deep in the Mississippi Delta, the cotton-rich flatland in northwest Mississippi that encompassed its poorest counties. Mississippi's black population faced a degree of poverty, ignorance, and political suppression unparalleled anywhere else in the United States. Eighty-six percent of all nonwhite families in the state lived below the national poverty level; their average annual income of $1,444 was the lowest in the country. The average Mississippi white made 200 percent more. Only 7 percent of Mississippi blacks finished twelve years of school, compared to 42 percent of the state's whites. Expenditures on white pupils were four times those for blacks across the state; in some rural counties the differential was as great as 4,000 percent. Only 5 percent of eligible blacks were registered to vote; in several counties there was not a single black registrant.[1] Local white attitudes were summed up in the motto of the White Citizens Councils,

"States Rights and Separation of the Races." The citizens councils ("country-club Klans") had helped elect Governor Ross Barnett and wielded immense political power in the state.

Amzie Moore was head of the Cleveland NAACP. Like Medgar Evers, head of the Mississippi NAACP, Moore had come back from fighting World War II infused with a fierce desire for political equality. Evers described how he felt when an armed mob obstructed him from voting: "I had been on Omaha Beach. All we wanted to be was ordinary citizens. We fought during the war for America, Mississippi included. Now, after the Germans and the Japanese hadn't killed us, it looked as though the white Mississippians would."[2] Moore organized resistance to a murderous terror campaign that met the returning black veterans. He was not much interested in integration—what good were integrated bus lines and lunch counters to sharecroppers who couldn't afford to use them? Moore told Moses to send some students to help blacks register to vote; promising that if they voted they would gain a lot more than bus rides and coffee. Moses promised to return.

To enlist the poorest, most remote, most endangered of America's citizens as participants in democracy—this was the goal from which SNCC would evolve, and America along with it. SNCC became the most revolutionary of the civil rights organizations, eventually calling not just for Christian justice but also for a complete realignment of power in America. As a result, SNCC also became the most feared of the civil rights groups. The conservative columnists Rowland Evans and Robert Novak liked to call it the "Nonstudent Violent Coordinating Committee." SNCC would change from an association of students to a corps of professional organizers, but the former students remained seekers of knowledge—self-exploring and confessional, experimental, iconoclastic. SNCC members would always insist that personal change accompany political change.

Ernest Noble, a black dry cleaner in McComb, Mississippi, where Robert Moses set up his first voter-registration outpost, recalled: "Poor Bob took a lot of beatings. . . . I just couldn't understand what Bob Moses was. Sometimes I think he was Moses in the Bible. He pioneered the way for black people in McComb. . . . He had more guts than any one man I've ever known."[3] He also had a Socratic, confessional way of guiding discussions at SNCC meetings. More often than not, it was Moses who could point to one among the diverging avenues that all could walk together.

In November 1961 Moses wrote a famous letter while serving a four-month jail sentence:

> We are smuggling this note from the drunk tank of the county jail in Magnolia Mississippi. Twelve of us are here, sprawled out along the concrete bunker . . . four veterans of the bunker are sitting up talking—mostly about girls. . . .

PREVIOUS PAGE: AT JAMES CHANEY'S FUNERAL: HIS MOTHER, FANNIE LEE CHANEY, AND HIS BROTHER BEN. **KENNETH THOMPSON**

Later on Hollis [Watkins] will lead out with a clear tenor into a freedom song; [Robert] Talbert and [Ike] Lewis will supply jokes; and [SNCC chairman Charles] McDew will discourse on the history of the black man and the Jew. McDew—a black by birth, a Jew by choice and a revolutionary by necessity—has taken on the deep hates and deep loves which America, and the world, reserve for those who dare to stand in the strong sun and cast a sharp shadow. . . .

It's mealtime now: we have rice and gravy in a flat pan, dry bread, and a "big town cake"; we lack eating and drinking utensils. Water comes from a faucet and goes into a hole.

This is Mississippi, the middle of the iceberg. Hollis is leading off with his tenor, "Michael, row the boat ashore, Alleluia; Christian brothers don't be slow, Alleluia; Mississippi's next to go, Alleluia." This is a tremor in the middle of the iceberg—a stone that the builders rejected.[4]

By the fall of 1962 Moses oversaw six offices and twenty field secretaries in Mississippi. Funds for these operations were coming from northern foundations, channeled through the Southern Regional Council's Voter Education Project (VEP). Amzie Moore's house became the headquarters of the Delta-region activities. Moses described the methods of the voter-registration cadres: "You dig into yourself and into the community to wage psychological warfare, you combat your own fears about beatings, shootings and possible mob violence; you stymie, by your mere physical presence, the anxious fear of the Negro community. . . . you organize, pound by pound, small bands of people. . . . you create a small striking force. . . . The deeper the fear, the deeper the problems in the community, the longer you have to stay to convince them."[5]

In July 1962 Moses sent twenty-three-year-old Sam Block, a Cleveland native who had been influenced by Moore, to organize in Greenwood—seat of Leflore County, the "Long-Staple Cotton Capital of the World." Block developed contacts in the community, called meetings, and found people willing to go down to the courthouse to try registering. To investigate a brutal beating of fourteen-year-old Welton McSwine in the police station, he took affidavits and photographed the boy's wounds, then sent his evidence to the Justice Department. "From then on," said Moses, "it was Sam versus the police."[6] His first time at the courthouse, accompanied by seven or eight aspiring registrants, Block had this public encounter:

SEE PAGE 148

The sheriff came up to me and he asked me, he said, "Nigger, where you from?" I told him, "Well, I'm a native Mississippian." He said, "Yeh, yeh, I know that, but . . . I know you ain't from here, 'cause I know every nigger and his mammy." I said, "Well, you know all the niggers, do you know any colored people?" He got angry. He spat in my face and walked. . . . So he came back and turned around and told me, "I don't want to see you in town any more. The best thing you better do is pack your clothes and get out and don't never come back no more." I said, "Well, sheriff, if you don't want to see me here, I think the best thing for you to do is pack your clothes and leave, get out of town, cause I'm here to stay, I came here to do a job and that is my intention, I'm going to do this job."[7]

Some days later, around midnight, Block was on the telephone with Moses when he realized that his Greenwood SNCC office was surrounded by men with guns and chains. Block knelt by the window, whispering into the phone. He didn't know what to do. Moses organized frantic calls to the Justice Department and the FBI. Hearing the rattle of chains coming up the stairs, Block and two fellow SNCC workers scrambled out a window, across roofs, and down a TV antenna. They hid with some friends in the community. Moses arrived at the Greenwood office with Willie Peacock at about 2:00 A.M. As Peacock remembered:

> He didn't see anything ruffled up or anything of that nature, so Bob turned the light on in the office, let the couch out and put the covers on, turned the fan on, which makes a lot of noise, and went to bed. I was very—I was scared. I just didn't understand what kind of guy this Bob Moses is, that could walk into a place where a lynch mob had just left and make up the bed and prepare to sleep, as if the situation was normal. So I guess I was learning, and I said, well, if Bob can go to sleep, I can go to sleep."[8]

That October, as James Meredith was taking his first classes in nearby Oxford, the supervisors of Leflore County decided to terminate the federal food-relief program that was keeping thousands of seasonally employed black farmers from starvation. SNCC then organized an effective relief drive, spearheaded by comedian Dick Gregory, with trucks and planes delivering tons of supplies from the North.

The relief drive was a funding and mobilization breakthrough for SNCC. "Friends of SNCC" offices—fund-raising and organizing affiliates in several large cities across the country—came alive for the effort. Northern urban supporters gained a new awareness of southern rural poverty. SNCC held a fund-raiser, headlined by Harry Belafonte, at Carnegie Hall on February 1, 1963, the third anniversary of the sit-in movement. The event inspired a new level of support for SNCC from black artists and from liberal and progressive northern whites. While organizing the concert SNCC broke the taboo against publicly accepting help from groups with Communist affiliations (even very old or innocent ties). As James Forman, SNCC's executive secretary, wrote: "By accepting the support of radicals and progressives, we helped to create an atmosphere that made it possible for many people scared by McCarthyism to come out of the woodwork and engage once again in active struggle. SNCC's role in helping to create a climate for radical thought and

SEE PAGE 184

action was an important contribution, in my opinion. It was one more way in which SNCC helped to accelerate the course of history."[9]

The Leflore relief drive had a historic impact on the Delta as well. While SNCC was feeding the county's poor it was also politicizing them, and it mobilized entire black communities, gaining trust by providing food and clothing along with political information and organization. Field secretaries taught the political relationship between starving children and unregistered parents; they made it clear that they were mainly interested in helping those who would help themselves onto the rolls of registered voters. Instead of twos or threes, now scores of blacks were attending mass meetings and were gathering at the courthouse to register.

On February 20, the day after nine thousand pounds of food and clothing arrived there from Chicago, the Greenwood SNCC office received an anonymous phone call from someone who gloated that no relief packages would be handed out the next day. As he spoke, four buildings in the black business district, one of them adjacent to the SNCC office, were burning to the ground. When Sam Block told the press that SNCC had been the target of a burnout, he was arrested for "public utterances designed to incite breach of the peace." More than a hundred local blacks demonstrated at Block's trial four days later; several hundred gathered for a mass meeting that evening. When some 150 blacks turned out to register over the next two days, it became the largest Mississippi registration drive since Reconstruction. "This is a new dimension," Moses wrote to the Chicago Friends of SNCC. "Negroes have never stood en masse in protest at the seat of power in the iceberg of Mississippi politics. . . . We don't know this plateau at all. We are relieved at the absence of immediate violence at the courthouse, but who knows what's to come next?"[10]

On the evening of February 28 a meeting was held in the Greenwood SNCC office; included were Moses and Randolph Blackwell of the Voter Education Project, who had been sent down to investigate the successful mobilization. SNCC volunteer Jimmy Travis interrupted to point out three white men parked outside in a Buick stripped of its license plates. The decision was made to break up the meeting; Moses, Blackwell, and Travis cautiously drove toward Sunflower County. Outside of town Travis, the driver, picked up the pursuing Buick in his rearview mirror. After a desperate chase down dark back roads, Travis was shot in the shoulder and neck; somehow Moses managed to steer the car off the road. Miraculously, in a operation at University Hospital in Jackson, Travis survived the removal of a bullet from his spinal cord.

"This can no longer be tolerated. We are accordingly today announcing a concentrated saturation campaign to register every qualified Negro in Leflore County," wrote Wiley Branton, head of the VEP, in a telegram to President Kennedy that was published in the *New York Times*.[11] As dozens of organizers from SNCC, the SCLC, and CORE poured into town, Greenwood's white community became crazed by fears of black political control. One resident told a *New York Times* reporter: "We killed two-month-old Indian babies to take this country, and now they want us to give it away to the niggers."[12]

The battle of Greenwood continued. Sam Block, Willie Peacock, Essie Broom, and Peggie Marye were parked outside the SNCC office when they were blasted by a shotgun; fortunately, the shots had been fired at such close range that they didn't spread out enough to cause serious wounds. On March 24 arsonists—this time with the right address—burned down the SNCC office. On March 26 buckshot was fired into the home of the Greene family. Dewey Greene Sr., a painter and paperhanger; Dewey Junior, who had applied to be the second black scholar at the University of Mississippi; his brother George; and their sisters Freddie and Alma were at the core of the Greenwood protest community. The attack on their home made friends and neighbors ready for stepped-up action, whatever its consequences. Bob Moses and James Forman led a group of 150 demonstrators to the city hall and courthouse, where they were halted by a squad of policemen. Moses and another demonstrator, Matthew Hughes, were set upon by a police dog (this a month before the famous dog attacks in Birmingham). Hughes was hospitalized; Moses, Forman, and other SNCC staffers were arrested. Forman, publicity wise, was exultant that he had managed to photograph the dog attack and secure the film before his arrest. One of his pictures was printed in the *Times*, prompting President Kennedy to demand that something be done.

The SNCC staffers were sentenced to four months in jail. The Justice Department negotiated a deal: in exchange for the release of the prisoners, the department would drop a federal lawsuit demanding protection for registrants in Greenwood. Moses was deeply depressed by the deal, believing that it had cut short the Greenwood momentum, a momentum that should have resulted in continuous federal presence and the eventual registration of large numbers of black voters in Mississippi.

SNCC members came to feel that the Kennedy administration's support of voting rights was always going to be betrayed by its reluctance to alienate southern authorities. SNCC pondered the weaknesses of the pending civil rights bill. The group's fourth general conference, in April 1963, yielded a new goal, which John Lewis summarized in his controversial March on Washington speech: "As it stands now, the voting section of this bill will not help the thousands of black people who want to vote. It will not help the citizens of Mississippi, of Alabama, and Georgia who are qualified to vote but lack a sixth grade education. 'One man, one vote,' is the African cry. It is ours, too. It must be ours. Let us tell the Congress: One man, one vote."[13]

"Like South Africa, only a little bit better." That was Allard Lowenstein's take on Mississippi, which he first visited to attend a demonstration marking Medgar Evers's assassination.[14] Lowenstein—former president of the National Student Association, later dean of students at Stanford University, then a congressman from New York and a leading antiwar activist—made plans with Bob Moses to generate a Mississippi "Freedom Vote." In the November gubernatorial election, unregistered Mississippians were

SEE PAGE 148

encouraged to vote on "freedom ballots" for "freedom candidates." Aaron "Doc" Henry, an NAACP leader from the Delta, ran for governor; Ed King, a white chaplain from Tougaloo College in Jackson, for lieutenant governor. Moses was their campaign manager.

Despite beatings and other harassments of organizers and voters, the Freedom Vote was a victory. Lowenstein brought in about sixty Stanford and Yale students to help organize the vote. The whole operation was run by the Council of Federated Organizations (COFO), an organization set up to channel funding mainly to SNCC but also to CORE and the NAACP in Mississippi. Over eighty thousand votes (out of a black adult population of five hundred thousand) were cast, at churches, beauty parlors, and streetside tables. SNCC's Ivanhoe Donaldson, who was arrested in Greenwood during the Freedom Vote, concluded: "It showed the Negro population that politics is not just 'white folks' business, but that Negroes are also capable of holding political offices. It introduced a lot of Negroes, for the first time, to the idea of marking ballots. For the first time, since Reconstruction, Negroes held a rally on the steps of the Courthouse, with their own candidates, expressing their own beliefs and ideas rather than those of the 'white folks.'"[15]

The success of the Freedom Vote inspired planning for the Mississippi Summer Project of 1964. This time, there would be a massive statewide campaign to garner real votes for real alternative electors at the Democratic National Convention. The Mississippi Freedom Democratic Party (MFDP) was established to challenge the whites-only regular Mississippi Democratic Party. One thousand white northern volunteers would be sought to help register voters, run "Freedom Schools," and set up community centers.

The idea of importing so many northern volunteers was fiercely debated among COFO and SNCC staffers. They worried over the contradictions inherent in employing privileged whites to teach self-empowerment to impoverished blacks. During the Freedom Vote the media had focused on the "Yalies" and ignored the other participants—a dismissal that appalled the veterans. Some noted the way educated white workers tended to "take over." On the other hand, as children of the elite, the volunteers would bring access to the media and to politicians. Moses believed that the presence of so many "outside agitators" would fan Mississippi to a "white heat"; the federal government might then be forced to step in, if only to protect the telegenic white volunteers, especially since it was an election year. The debate ended when SNCC's Executive Committee eventually adopted former chairman Marion Barry's somewhat indefinite motion "to obtain the right for all citizens of Mississippi to vote, using as many people as necessary to obtain that end."[16]

Most of the volunteers were from elite northern universities. They filled out questionnaires and were vetted by interviewers looking to weed out the uncommitted and those not strong enough to withstand the coming hardships and dangers. Each volunteer had to pledge a $500 bond against possible arrest and to pay for transportation and living expenses. They were asked to provide the names and addresses of their local news publications and media contacts, and they also had to supply four copies of a portrait photograph to be filed for use by the Summer Project's Communications office.

Over eight hundred volunteers gathered for training in Oxford, Ohio. Moses, director of the Mississippi Summer Project, told them things like: "When Mrs. Hamer sang, 'If you miss me from the freedom fight, and you can't find me anywhere; Come on over to the graveyard, I'll be buried over there.' . . . That's true."[17] Such warnings of danger mixed with freedom songs, idealistic confessions, and a sense of history in the making— intensified by the presence of reporters from the national media at every lecture and bull session—combined to produce a feeling of ecstasy that was called a "freedom high."

On Saturday, June 20, CORE employees Michael Schwerner and Ben Chaney drove a carload of fresh trainees toward their posts in Meridian, Mississippi's second largest city. As they drove down they could have heard Governor Ross Barnett proclaim on the radio: "Mississippi has been made the special target of the Communists and the Mixers because Mississippi has given the nation and the world the shining example of successful segregation."[18] The civil rights bill being debated in Congress and the Freedom Summer "invasion" gave white Mississippians the sense of being at war with the rest of America.

Michael Schwerner ran the small Meridian CORE office with his wife, Rita. Schwerner had worked part-time for CORE while doing social work in Manhattan's Lower East Side. "What caused him to want to go South was Birmingham," a coworker recalled. "He had been deeply affected by the photographs of Negroes sprawling under the dogs and the fire hoses."[19] Mickey (also called "Mitch" because of his Mitch Miller goatee) and Rita had been hired as CORE field secretaries, salaried at $9.80 per week each. In charge of six counties, Mickey Schwerner was the highest-ranking white man in the Mississippi movement. He managed to get a dedicated local volunteer, James Chaney, onto the CORE payroll as well. And at Oxford, Schwerner picked a fellow New York Jew, Andrew Goodman, to run a project in Neshoba County.

After touring the Meridian office and grabbing a couple hours of sleep, Schwerner, Chaney, and Goodman set out for Longdale, in Neshoba County. It was Sunday, June 21, Father's Day and the longest day of the year. After its congregation volunteered to house a freedom school, Mount Zion Methodist Church in Longdale had been burned to the ground by the Ku Klux Klan. Schwerner wanted to inspect the scene and reassure the parishioners without delay. It was a risky mission, and they alerted the office staff to start searching for them if they did not return by 4:00 P.M.

The three were arrested a few hours later in Neshoba County, incarcerated in the county jailhouse, and released in the middle of the night. They never returned. It soon became obvious that they had been murdered. President Lyndon B. Johnson met with the parents of the two white victims and sent two hundred U.S. sailors to help find the bodies. The disappearances were such major news that the uproar helped end a southern fili-buster in Congress against the proposed civil rights act and eased its passage, on July 2.

SEE PAGE 154

An informant, bribed by a reported thirty thousand dollars, eventually divulged the triple-burial site. The bodies were unearthed on August 4. An autopsy found that all three had been shot in the head and that Chaney had been brutally beaten. Pathologist Dr. David Spain wrote, "I felt every fiber in my own body shaking, as I involuntarily imagined the scene at the time this youngster received such a vicious beating to shatter his bones in this incredible manner."[20] These three civil rights workers—white and black, northern and southern, seasoned and virginal—became the best-known martyrs of the movement.

Their murderers were never convicted. William Bradford Huie, the same journalist who had investigated the Till murder, spoke to some of the conspirators. Huie believed that "perhaps as many as forty citizens of Mississippi spent Sunday evening committing . . . a planned murder for the purpose of dramatizing Mississippi's defiance of the laws of the United States! . . . It was part of a continuing war between Mississippi terrorists and the United States of America."[21]

The disappearances, on the very first day of Freedom Summer, led off a cruel and angry season in Mississippi. During the Neshoba County search, three other corpses of lynched black men turned up. As the summer progressed, another project worker was killed, four were critically wounded, eighty were beaten. There were over a thousand arrests of project workers, and over sixty bombings or burnings of movement-related black churches, homes, or businesses. The Mississippi violence filled both new volunteers and experienced civil rights workers with fear and rage and determination. It was the "longest nightmare of my life," wrote SNCC veteran Cleveland Sellers.[22] The violence exacerbated tensions between coworkers of different races, classes, and genders. Fear—and pragmatism—undercut the appeal of nonviolence; armed self-defense among SNCC workers was becoming an open secret.

Despite the violence, the three main activities of Freedom Summer continued: canvassing for MFDP ballots, establishing freedom schools, and running community centers. Over two thousand students attended forty-one freedom schools, whose curricula emphasized personal awareness and political participation. There is much testimony that teachers, students, and parents were changed for life by these classes. The freedom schools embodied the notion that any community could develop a practical, unofficial educational system within a hostile environment. The freedom school experiments of that summer would influence many later educational developments, including the Head Start program.

On the voter-registration front, about eighty thousand blacks were enrolled in the MFDP. Originally planned as a purely symbolic gesture of defiance against the exclusionary white Mississippi Democratic Party, the MFDP was transformed by the Freedom Summer events into a real challenger at the Democratic National Convention. The delegates who traveled to Atlantic City in August were supported by various liberal factions of the

SEE PAGE 157

Democratic Party. The battle over whether or not they would be recognized became the salient event of the convention.

Fannie Lou Hamer, a leading MFDP delegate, testified to the Credentials Committee —and to several million Americans watching live television coverage of the proceedings. She spoke about her attempts to become a registered voter in the Delta, about her subsequent eviction from her job and home, about being tortured in a Mississippi jail. "Is this America, the land of the free and the home of the brave, where we are threatened daily because we want to live as decent human beings?" Mrs. Hamer asked. Apprised of the power of her appeals, President Johnson called an impromptu news conference, which succeeded in luring away the network coverage—though the evening's prime-time newscasts replayed extensive excerpts from Mrs. Hamer's impassioned speech. Johnson's main concern was getting the southern votes he needed to become president. After Governor George Wallace's stunning showings in the Democratic primaries—he took 30 to 40 percent of the votes in Wisconsin, Indiana, and Maryland—Johnson could no longer take the election for granted. He pasted together a compromise proposal that would have recognized two of the MFDP delegates (instead of the full delegation of forty-one). Most civil rights leaders endorsed the plan as a symbolic victory, but it was rejected by the MFDP delegation as offensively patronizing. Some thought the terms were crafted expressly to keep Mrs. Hamer out of the convention.

The Atlantic City defeat radically changed SNCC. As Cleveland Sellers wrote: "Never again were we lulled into believing that our task was exposing injustices so that 'good' people of America could eliminate them. We left Atlantic City with the knowledge that the movement had turned into something else. After Atlantic City, our struggle was not for civil rights, but for liberation."[23]

Freedom Summer transformed those who participated in it and transformed America. It had a profound impact on later activism in America. Many forms of "the counterculture" originated during Freedom Summer—communal living ("freedom houses"); politicized experimental sexuality ("free love"); interracial relationships; and jeans and workshirts (the "SNCC uniform"). Volunteers (aside from the eighty or so who stayed on) went back to their campuses and communities radicalized by their experiences of Mississippi "justice," empowered by their successes, and haloed in media glory. Many became student leaders who would guide the subsequent movements of the 1960s.[24]

One Freedom Summer volunteer, Mario Savio, who had shown few signs of leadership before his southern stint, led the Berkeley Free Speech Movement of 1964, the seminal white student uprising of the 1960s. Savio said in a famous speech: "Last summer I went to Mississippi to join the struggle there for civil rights. This fall I am engaged in another phase of the same struggle, this time in Berkeley. The two battlefields may seem quite different to some observers, but . . . the same rights are at stake in both places—the right to participate as citizens in democratic society and the right to due process of law."[25]

The first massive student demonstrations against the Vietnam War, the "teach-ins" of the spring of 1965, were organized, in part, by Freedom Summer alumni at the University of Michigan. In 1967 the Resistance, a leading national antiwar organization, was founded by Mississippi veterans, with Summer Project experiences foremost on their minds. The Vietnam Summer Project of 1967, "the largest organizing effort the New Left ever attempted," was modeled on Freedom Summer and was staffed by many former volunteers.[26]

At the November 1964 SNCC conference that followed Freedom Summer, two white female staffers, Mary King and Casey Hayden, circulated a position paper protesting the demeaning treatment of women workers in SNCC. King, who drafted the statement, was codirector, with Julian Bond, of the SNCC Communications office. She was the first to articulate the blatant discrepancy between SNCC's stated beliefs in equality and the functioning hierarchy that placed black men at the top, followed by white men, white women, and finally black women at the bottom. Stokely Carmichael's infamous response was "the position of women in SNCC is prone." Some historians date the beginning of the 1960s women's movement to a follow-up article by King and Hayden, published in *Liberation* in April 1966. Many of the organizers of the first women's liberation groups were Freedom Summer alumni. Some have spoken of their involvement in the women's movement as an attempted return to that experience: "What I remember about Mississippi was the love I felt . . . from everyone. There was this openness and acceptance of you as a person that I've never really felt since, not even in the women's movement, even though that's what we were trying to recreate."[27]

SNCC and the Freedom Summer Project practiced an existential politics of the personal in action. They taught a new kind of activism and a new way of life to an entire generation. The movements that came later in the 1960s—the black power movement, the peace movement, the student movement, the women's movement, the environmental movement, the gay rights movement, the alternative-education movement, and others—were all their progeny.

"JULIAN BOND AND MEMBERS OF THE STUDENT
NONVIOLENT COORDINATING COMMITTEE, ATLANTA,
GEORGIA, MARCH 23, 1963." **RICHARD AVEDON**

Julian Bond (center), SNCC's communications director, is flanked by Robert Zellner, SNCC's first white field secretary, and by Dorothy Miller Zellner, who had been hired by SNCC chairman James Forman to work with Bond on publicity and on SNCC's newspaper, the *Student Voice.*

A variant of this picture is the concluding image in Avedon and James Baldwin's book *Nothing Personal* (1964), where it is accompanied by this text: "The sea rises, the light fails, lovers cling to each other, and children cling to us. The moment we cease to hold each other, the moment we break faith with one another, the sea engulfs us and the light goes out."

Avedon trained several SNCC photographers in his New York studio. After he told Marty Forscher, who ran a famous camera-repair shop, how much they needed equipment, supplies, and service, Forscher (with the help of sympathetic clients and friends) sent film and over seventy-five cameras down South over a three-year period—a creative gesture of financial support that made possible much of the movement photography. "It seemed to be a wonderful way to put my money where my mouth was."

POLICEMEN, CLARKSDALE, MISSISSIPPI, FALL 1963.
DANNY LYON

"The Clarksdale, Mississippi, police pose for a photograph as ministers from the National Council of Churches march to the local church." (Lyon's caption.)

Southern civil rights groups occasionally invited northern white clergymen to visit, for their support and their publicity value. During the Freedom Summer of 1964, COFO coordinated the participation of over three hundred ministers representing the National Council of Churches.

OPPOSITE: BACKYARD OF THE SNCC OFFICE, GREENWOOD, MISSISSIPPI, JULY 8, 1963. **DANNY LYON**

"After giving a concert in a cotton field in Greenwood, Bob Dylan plays behind the SNCC office. Bernice Reagon, one of the original Freedom Singers and today leader of Sweet Honey in the Rock, listens. Mendy Sampstein sits behind Dylan and talks to Willie Blue." (Lyon's caption.)

This concert, which also featured Theodore Bikel and Pete Seeger, was held in support of the Greenwood voter-registration drive.

RIGHT: SNCC POSTER ON THE FRONT PORCH OF A HOUSE, RULEVILLE, MISSISSIPPI, 1965 OR 1966. **BOB FLETCHER**

This poster is a Danny Lyon photograph of demonstrators singing at the March on Washington.

Bob Fletcher took up photography while working with the Harlem Education Project (HEP) in 1963. The first time he went out to photograph a street action—a rent-strike protest—he was arrested; while in jail he decided to move down South, where the risks would be "more significant." He was accepted as a freedom school teacher in the Mississippi Summer Project and later replaced Tamio Wakayama in SNCC's Atlanta darkroom.

RALLY FOR FREEDOM VOTE CANDIDATES, HINDS COUNTY
COURTHOUSE, JACKSON, MISSISSIPPI, FALL 1963.
MATT HERRON

The Freedom Vote, or Freedom Ballot Campaign, was a chance for unregistered black voters to practice voting in a mock election. Aaron "Doc" Henry (front row, left) was the candidate for governor, Ed King (second row, bandaged), for lieutenant governor. Sam Block and Willie Peacock of SNCC are in the front row, center.

Campaigners were subjected to intense harassment. In Adams County, SNCC field secretary George Greene and volunteer Bruce Payne (a Yale graduate student) were shot at, but they managed to escape by driving 105 miles an hour down the wrong side of the road. Payne later asked Ed King, "Do you think those fellows really intended to kill us? Those bullets really hit the car sorta low." King replied, "In Mississippi it is an error to confuse good intentions with poor aim."

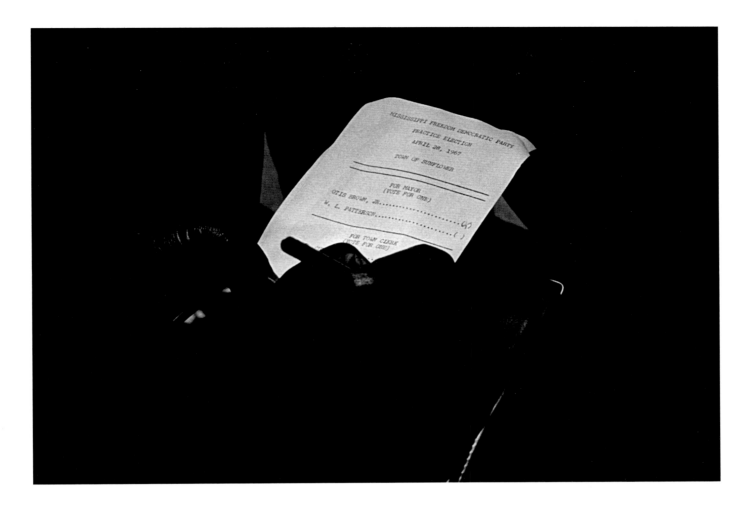

VOTING IN AN MFDP PRACTICE ELECTION, SUNFLOWER
COUNTY, MISSISSIPPI, APRIL 28, 1967. **MARIA VARELA**

Varela writes: "I was there, most likely, in Sunflower to continue to take photos which would be used in 'how to' books
and filmstrips that I put together at organizers' requests. I
was SNCC staff during this period, but I was responding to
requests for help with photos and educational materials
from MFDP, COFO, and SNCC organizers."

Varela has recently been awarded the prestigious Mac-
Arthur Fellowship for her work organizing co-op movements
in rural New Mexico communities.

EDIE BLACK TEACHES A FREEDOM SCHOOL CLASS IN
MILESTON, MISSISSIPPI, A COMMUNITY OF INDEPENDENT
BLACK FARMERS, SUMMER 1964. **MATT HERRON**

Pam Parker, a freedom school volunteer teacher, wrote in a letter: "The atmosphere in the class is unbelievable. It is what every teacher dreams about—real, honest enthusiasm and desire to learn anything and everything. The girls come to class of their own free will. They respond to everything that is said. They are excited about learning. They drain me of everything that I have to offer so that I go home at night completely exhausted but very happy in spirit because I know that I have given to people."

Photojournalist Matt Herron initiated the Southern Documentary Project during the Freedom Summer of 1964. The project set out to go beyond the confines of "demo-oriented" photojournalistic coverage of the movement while remaining free of direct movement sponsorship. The Southern Documentary Project enlisted photographers Herron, George Ballis, Fred de Van, Nick Lawrence, Danny Lyon, Norris McNamara, Dave Prince, and Maria Varela—a mix of professional photojournalists, independent documentarians, and activists with photographic skills. Howard Chapnick, president of the Black Star photo agency in New York, distributed the pictures and even secured some stipends from *Life* (which received, in return, the right of first refusal on the project's pictures).

COFO FREEDOM HOUSE IN THE MISSISSIPPI DELTA,
SUMMER 1964. **TAMIO WAKAYAMA**

The cross in front of Freedom House was burnt there by the Klan. It was left in place, inscribed by COFO members with the countermessage "Freedom."

The Canadian Tamio Wakayama joined SNCC after reading about the Sixteenth Street Baptist Church bombing. He bunked with John Lewis and Danny Lyon in Atlanta, where he worked on SNCC publications and printed in the SNCC darkroom. He began to take photographs after Danny Lyon lent him a Nikon.

BELOW: FBI CIRCULAR ISSUED JUNE 29, 1964, DEPICTING THE THREE CIVIL RIGHTS WORKERS WHO DISAPPEARED NEAR PHILADELPHIA, MISSISSIPPI, ON JUNE 21, 1964. **UNITED PRESS INTERNATIONAL**

"WASHINGTON—FBI Director J. Edgar Hoover reported to Pres. Johnson 6/29 that the search for three missing civil rights workers in Mississippi had been expanded to five states and that he was distributing thousands of circulars (copy of one shown here) in Mississippi, Alabama, Tennessee, Arkansas, and Louisiana. Initial search was confined to the area around Philadelphia, Miss." (Original UPI caption.)

Six weeks after their disappearance, an informant—reportedly paid thirty thousand dollars—led federal agents to the bodies of Chaney, Goodman, and Schwerner, buried in the dam of a newly constructed cattle pond.

RIGHT: THE BURNED-OUT STATION WAGON DRIVEN BY JAMES CHANEY, ANDREW GOODMAN, AND MICHAEL SCHWERNER, BOGUE CHITTO CREEK, NESHOBA COUNTY, MISSISSIPPI, JUNE 23, 1964. **STEVE SCHAPIRO**

Two days after Chaney, Goodman, and Schwerner disappeared, FBI agents found the burned remains of their vehicle in a swamp off secluded roads. President Lyndon B. Johnson ordered in 200 navy men to search for the civil rights workers' bodies. During the search three other bodies were found—all lynching victims whose murderers were never brought to trial.

ABOVE, LEFT: ROBERT GOODMAN COMFORTS HIS WIFE, CAROLINE, UPON THE ARRIVAL OF THEIR SON'S BODY AT NEWARK AIRPORT, AUGUST 7, 1964. **UNITED PRESS INTERNATIONAL**

ABOVE, RIGHT: DAVID DENNIS SPEAKING AT JAMES CHANEY'S FUNERAL, MERIDIAN, MISSISSIPPI, AUGUST 8, 1964. **GEORGE BALLIS**

David Dennis, the chief CORE organizer during the Mississippi Summer Project, broke into furious tears as he delivered his eulogy for James Chaney: "Your work is just beginning. If you go back home and sit down and take what these white men in Mississippi are doing to us . . . if you take it and don't do something about it . . . then God damn your souls."

OPPOSITE: ROBERT MOSES SPEAKING AT A MEMORIAL SERVICE FOR CHANEY, GOODMAN, AND SCHWERNER, LONGDALE, MISSISSIPPI, AUGUST 16, 1964. **TAMIO WAKAYAMA**

On the day of their murders the three civil rights workers had driven to Longdale to inspect the remains of Mount Zion Methodist Church, which had been torched by the Klan. Bob Moses, head of the Mississippi Summer Project, addressed a memorial gathering held exactly two months after the fire: "The tragedy here is the work of people who believed in an idea enough to kill for it. The problem of Mississippi is the problem of the nation and the world. A way has to be found to change this desire to kill."

ARRAIGNMENT OF TWENTY MEN ON CHARGES OF
CONSPIRING TO MURDER, MERIDIAN, MISSISSIPPI,
DECEMBER 4, 1964. **BILL REED**

Front row right is Philadelphia sheriff Lawrence Rainey;
left is Deputy Cecil Price, who had arrested Chaney, Goodman, and Schwerner prior to their murders. The charges at
this arraignment were dismissed, but in 1967 Price and
nine others were convicted of federal conspiracy charges
and received jail terms of from three to ten years.

FANNIE LOU HAMER AT THE DEMOCRATIC NATIONAL
CONVENTION, ATLANTIC CITY, AUGUST 22–26, 1964.
KENNETH THOMPSON

The youngest of sixteen children born to a family of share-croppers, Fannie Lou Hamer was a leader of the Mississippi Freedom Democratic Party (MFDP), which challenged the all-white official delegation. She came to prominence during her televised testimony at a convention hearing about her life and political struggles. Julius Lester has written:

> When Mrs. Fannie Lou Hamer testified before the cre-dentials committee of the Convention, her testimony

was so eloquent and so moving that crooked congress-men were crying, and then suddenly, "We interrupt this program for a special announcement from the President of the United States." And Big Lyndon himself came on with some jive announcement about why the price of collard greens was going up or something and kept say-ing it until Mrs. Hamer had finished her testimony. Nonetheless, the MFDP dominated convention activities.

BELOW: ELLA BAKER ADDRESSING A RALLY OF THE
MISSISSIPPI FREEDOM DEMOCRATIC PARTY OUTSIDE THE
DEMOCRATIC NATIONAL CONVENTION. **GEORGE BALLIS**

Ella Baker played several crucial roles in the civil rights movement. She was an early director of the SCLC. In 1960 she was instrumental in unifying the scattered student sit-in crews into a coherent national student movement, SNCC. In 1964 she helped form COFO and the MFDP.

Behind Baker is a poster of Michael Schwerner, whose body had been unearthed some two weeks before; his murder, and all it symbolized, was a major issue for the MFDP and the convention.

OPPOSITE: PLACARDS OF GOODMAN, CHANEY, AND
SCHWERNER AT A DEMONSTRATION ON THE BOARDWALK
DURING THE DEMOCRATIC NATIONAL CONVENTION.
BOB FLETCHER

Sally Belfrage ends her book *Freedom Summer* with this recollection of Fannie Lou Hamer's leading a round of "We Shall Overcome" on the boardwalk outside the convention:

The song begins slowly . . . just a song, the last one, before we separate. You see the others, and the instant when it comes to each one to think what the words mean, when each nearly breaks, wondering: shall we overcome?

The hands hold each other tighter. Mrs. Hamer is smiling, flinging out the words, and crying at once. "Black and white together," she leads the next verse and a sort of joy begins to grow in every face; "We are not afraid"— and for just that second no one is afraid, because they are free.

ABOVE: SIGNING THE CIVIL RIGHTS ACT,
JULY 1964. **UNITED PRESS INTERNATIONAL**

President Johnson shakes hands with Martin Luther
King, Jr. Between them is Senator Jacob Javits.

RIGHT: MARTIN LUTHER KING, JR., IN A
MOTORCADE IS THRONGED BY SUPPORTERS,
BALTIMORE, OCTOBER 31, 1964. **LEONARD FREED**

In mid-October 1964 Martin Luther King, Jr., was
recovering from exhaustion in an Atlanta hospital
when he learned that he had won the Nobel Peace
Prize. At thirty-five, he was the youngest recipient
ever. On October 21 King set out on a nationwide
voter-turnout drive. He supported the campaign of
President Johnson, telling a Baltimore rally that
"[Republican candidate Barry] Goldwater is a threat
to freedom." Leaflets were circulated calling for
write-in votes for King; the day before the election
King publicly denounced the leaflets as a Republican dirty trick designed to siphon black votes from
the Democrats.

7

SELMA, 1965

"We Must Go to Montgomery and See the King"

Selma, Alabama, the quiet seat of Dallas County, is about an hour's drive west of the state capital, Montgomery. To enter Selma you pass a strip of gas stations, car dealerships, and fast-food joints, then cross the Alabama River on a dramatic steel arch, the Edmund Pettus Bridge, named after a Confederate general. During Reconstruction, Pettus had testified before the U.S. Congress's Joint Select Committee investigating Ku Klux Klan activities in Alabama and denied the existence of any such "bands" in his county. As for those that might exist elsewhere, he expressed only contempt for their ungentlemanly upbringing and methods.[1]

"Dallas is the birthplace of the White Citizens Council in the State of Alabama. It is also the Stronghold of the Ku Klux Klan," noted Bernard Lafayette in a SNCC field report from Selma, written shortly after he and his wife, Colia, were posted there in February 1963.[2] The Lafayettes were welcomed by one of Selma's few black voters, Amelia Boynton, an insurance agent and a leader of the Dallas County Voters' League. Despite the courageous efforts of the league and the NAACP, only about 1 percent of Dallas County blacks had been able to register. No surprise, given that the registration office was open only two days per month, on Monday. During the brief periods when the registrars were not out to lunch, they would subject any black applicant to endless forms and a grueling test of reading, writing, and knowledge of the Constitution.

Aided by Mrs. Boynton and other local stalwarts, the Lafayettes took on the task of shaking up Selma. They went to the Chicken Shack, the black Elks' Club, bars, and churches, handing out leaflets and inviting folk to voter-registration classes. They held

mass meetings. They dealt with harassment, firings from jobs, beatings, and arrests of prospective voters. They ran up against Dallas County sheriff James G. Clark, Jr.

Clark was a notoriously sadistic and racist "peacekeeper." His volunteer posse of over a hundred men rode into battle in cars and on horseback, carrying guns, whips, clubs, and electric cattle prods. Clark and his posse terrorized Dallas County and beyond, a self-appointed anti–civil rights squad, often working in concert with the state troopers under Colonel Al Lingo. Like Clark, Lingo (who had been appointed by his friend Governor George Wallace) tended toward violent excess.

On January 2, 1965, Sheriff Clark was in Miami for the Orange Bowl in which Alabama quarterback Joe Namath was most valuable player. In Selma that evening Nobel Laureate Martin Luther King, Jr. (recently named *Time* Man of the Year), addressed a large mass meeting. Gathered with him in Brown Chapel African Methodist Episcopal Church was a coalition of Selma blacks such as had never before been seen, a testimony to the long years of organizing by Amelia Boynton, the Lafayettes, and many others. With Clark out of town, his posse was kept under control by the newly appointed Selma police chief Wilson Baker, a relative moderate. King was inaugurating the SCLC's Alabama Project:

> At the rate they are letting us register now it will take a hundred and three years to register all of the fifteen thousand Negroes in Dallas County who are qualified to vote. . . . But we don't have that long to wait. . . . Today marks the beginning of a determined, organized, mobilized campaign to get the right to vote everywhere in Alabama. . . . Our cry to the State of Alabama is a simple one: *Give us the ballot.* . . . We are not on our knees begging for the ballot. *We are demanding the ballot.*[3]

The Alabama Project, centered on Selma and Dallas County, was a major campaign to secure effective federal protection of voting rights. That protection had been compromised out of the Civil Rights Act of 1964. Since Johnson's landslide defeat of Barry Goldwater in the 1964 election, the White House and the Justice Department had been discussing a new voting rights bill. King and other civil rights leaders were insisting on immediate, potent legislation that would install federal registrars whenever needed and that would ban all discriminatory poll tests.

The SCLC's Alabama plans were not secret. Wilson Baker remembered: "We had obtained them through some sources. . . . I have heard the story that Dr. King either lost his briefcase or some way it was misplaced in Anniston. . . . I think every law enforcement officer in the state had a copy of the thing."[4] They knew that the plan involved exposing the hair-trigger cruelty of Jim Clark and his posse.

PREVIOUS PAGE: ON THE SELMA TO MONTGOMERY MARCH, MARCH 21–25, 1965.
JAMES KARALES

On January 19, the second day of the SCLC's organized marches, Amelia Boynton was arrested by Clark in front of the county courthouse. A photograph of her being brutally manhandled ran the next day in the *Washington Post* and the *New York Times*. At a mass meeting Ralph Abernathy ironically nominated Clark to honorary membership in the Dallas County Voters' League—for publicity services rendered. Clark heard such remarks on surveillance tapes that he had made of these meetings. "He'd scream bloody murder that he'd never do it again, he wouldn't fall into that trap again and go out the next day and do the same thing," Baker recalled.[5]

On February 10 Clark tried to dislodge a group of about two hundred high schoolers protesting outside the courthouse. First he simply surrounded them with his scowling posse. At lunchtime he ostentatiously handed out fried chicken to his men, hoping that hunger pangs would break the youngsters' ranks. Then his patience ended. The posse pressed the teenagers into a "forced march" across town, down Water Street, and out beyond the city. Reporters and cameramen were kept away. Screaming, stumbling, panting, the kids were herded along by cattle prods, which delivered a fierce sting but left no scars. Some miles out of town, the march was terminated, the marchers left in ditches. Some were vomiting from exhaustion. Baker drove to the scene with two SNCC workers hidden in his car so that they could help bring the kids back to town. "I'm human too," he explained.[6] Even some of Selma's white citizens—not one of whom had ever before spoken up publicly against racial injustices—called for putting Clark on a tighter leash.

Two days later, in front of the courthouse and cameramen, the SCLC's C. T. Vivian told Clark, "You're racists in the same way that Hitler was a racist."[7] Clark (or his deputy) punched Vivian in the face with such force that he fractured a finger. Vivian was dragged off bleeding to jail. Clark checked into Vaughan Memorial Hospital the next day with chest pains. "The niggers are giving me a heart attack," he told a reporter.[8] Demonstrators prayed for Clark's health, "In Body and Mind," as one sign put it.

Upon his release from jail, Vivian drove thirty miles northwest to Marion to address a mass meeting. A night march from the church to the jail was planned, and the police were spreading rumors that James Orange, a popular SCLC field secretary, was going to be broken out of jail by the marchers. Police reinforcements were speeding in from all around the state. Richard Valeriani, a reporter for NBC News, recalled: "I went to Marion and the crowd was particularly nasty that night. A lot of townspeople had gathered around, and we knew we were in for trouble right away because people came up and started spraying the cameras with paint."[9]

Valeriani was clubbed to the ground. Albert Turner, a Marion leader, described what happened next:

> Probably one of the most vicious situations that was in the whole Civil Rights Movement. . . . One of the major things that was so bad that night, they shot the [street]

SEE PAGE 175

lights out, and nobody was able to report what really happened. . . . They beat people at random. They didn't have to be marching. All you had to do was be black. And they hospitalized probably fifteen or twenty folks. And they just was intending to kill somebody as an example, and they did kill Jimmie Jackson. . . . He was shot in the side that night and later died.[10]

Jimmie Lee Jackson, who was trying to protect his mother from a beating, was shot at point-blank range by an Alabama state trooper. His murder had the movement boiling with rage and determination. A Marion activist, Lucie Foster, called for a march to the state capital. There was talk of laying Jimmie Jackson's body at George Wallace's feet. James Bevel, pacing outside his room at the Torch Motel, had been struck by a similar notion. At a memorial service for Jackson on Sunday, February 28, Bevel floated his idea at the end of a fiery sermon. His text was from the Book of Esther, where Esther is charged to "go unto the king, to make supplication unto him, and to make request before him for her people." "I must go see the king!" Bevel shouted, "We must go to Montgomery and see the king!"[11]

Several days later Martin Luther King, Jr., confirmed that a march from Selma to Montgomery would take place. He met with President Johnson in Washington, D.C., on March 5, outlining his views on the proposed voting rights legislation. On Sunday, March 7, about six hundred marchers, perhaps half from Marion, assembled in Brown Chapel. The mood was somber. Dr. King had been kept away by his aides, who had been warned in the strongest terms by Attorney General Nicholas Katzenbach of credible threats to King's life. At the head of the march would be John Lewis, SNCC's national chairman, and the SCLC's Hosea Williams; they had won a coin toss with James Bevel and Andrew Young. Next in line would be Albert Turner of Marion and Robert Mants of Selma SNCC. Governor Wallace had vowed to stop the march as "not conducive to the orderly flow of traffic and commerce." The Medical Committee for Human Rights (MCHR) had prepared four rented ambulances and hearses to serve as first-aid vehicles.

As Lewis remembers it: "We did have little bags, knapsacks, and lunch or something like that, books to read along the way. But we hadn't set up tents along the way; we didn't have any place to stay. Apparently the idea was that we would march outside of Selma that night and then come back, and then the next morning we would continue."[12]

As the marchers crossed the hump of the Pettus Bridge just after 4:00 P.M., they could see the forces positioned at the bottom. They faced a blue wall of troopers, while a mounted posse and assorted thugs were lurking in the wings. The troopers had gas masks on their belts and were brandishing clubs. Al Lingo and Jim Clark pulled up in a car nearby.

"John, can you swim?" Williams asked Lewis. "No." "I can't either," said Williams, "and I'm sure we're gonna end up in that river." They led the marchers down to the line of troopers. The troopers donned their gas masks. Major John Cloud announced: "You are ordered to disperse, go home or to your church. This march will not continue.

SEE PAGE 177

You have two minutes." Williams said, "May we have a word with you, Major?" "There is no word to be had." After one minute, Cloud ordered, "Troopers, advance."[13]

> The troopers rushed forward, their blue uniforms and white helmets blurring into a flying wedge as they moved.
>
> The wedge moved with such force that it seemed almost to pass over the waiting column rather than through it.
>
> The first ten or twenty Negroes were swept to the ground screaming, arms and legs flying. . . .
>
> Those still on their feet retreated.
>
> The troopers continued pushing, using both the force of their bodies and the prodding of their nightsticks.
>
> A cheer went up from the white spectators lining the south side of the highway.
>
> The mounted possemen spurred their horses and rode at a run into the retreating mass. . . .
>
> Suddenly there was a report like a gunshot and a grey cloud spewed over the troopers and the Negroes.
>
> "Tear gas!" someone yelled.
>
> The cloud began covering the highway. . . .
>
> Fifteen or twenty nightsticks could be seen through the gas, flailing at the heads of the marchers.[14]

SEE PAGE 178

SEE PAGE 179

Lewis recalled: "I was hit. I was hit almost on the same spot I was hit on the Freedom Ride in 1961. . . . This trooper just kept hitting. But it was such a force. They were running . . . over anything that was standing, so I was literally knocked down and hit. I just felt like it was the beginning of the end. . . . It became difficult for me to breathe, and you just sorta felt, 'Just let me be.'"[15]

Sheyann Webb, an eight-year-old marcher, recollected: "I was runnin'. I was afraid, and Hosea picked me up, and I told him to put me down 'cause he was runnin' too slow. . . . Tears were splattered everywhere, and I ran all the way home."[16] Another marcher recalled: "They literally whipped folk all the way back to the church. They even came up in the yard of the church, hittin' on folk. Ladies, men, babies, children—they didn't give a damn who they were."[17]

The first-aid vehicles had been blockaded by the police at the city side of the bridge. Dr. Alfred Moldovan, who was leading the MCHR workers, pleaded with Baker to let them cross over to the wounded. At first the police chief threatened to blow the doctor's head off, but eventually he let the vehicles through.[18] "I recall," said Lewis, "several people that had been on the march assisted in getting me back [across the bridge]."[19] The nearly one hundred wounded were treated at several hospitals and makeshift first-aid centers. Lewis was hospitalized for three days with a brain concussion.

George B. Leonard wrote about his family's reactions to the beatings he saw on television:

> A shrill cry of terror, unlike any that had passed through a T.V. set, rose up as the troopers lumbered forward, stumbling sometimes on the fallen bodies. . . . Periodically the top of a helmeted head emerged from the cloud, followed by a club on the upswing. The club and the head would disappear into the cloud of gas and another club would bob up and down.
>
> *Unhuman.* No other word can describe the motions. . . . My wife, sobbing, turned and walked away, saying, "I can't look any more. . . ."
>
> I was not aware that at the same moment people all up and down the West Coast were feeling what my wife and I felt, that at various times all over the country . . . that night hundreds of these people would drop whatever they were doing, that some of them would leave home without clothes, borrow money, overdraw their checking accounts; board planes, buses, trains, cars; travel thousands of miles with no luggage . . . for a single purpose: to place themselves alongside the Negroes they had watched on television.[20]

Frederick Reese—minister, schoolteacher, president of the Dallas County Voters' League, and one of the primary organizers of the Selma actions—remembers being in Brown Chapel at about 11:00 P.M. on Bloody Sunday:

> You hear the door of the church opening and there is a group of people, black and white, who came in from New Jersey. They had chartered a plane. And they walked into the church, down the aisle to the front, and they said to us, "We are here to share with the people of Selma in this struggle for the right to vote. We have seen on the television screen the violence that took place today, and we're here to share it with you." There was a round of applause in the church and you could feel a change in the atmosphere— a spirit of inspiration, motivation, hope, coming back into the eyes and into the minds of these people—and then renewed commitment to the nonviolent method.[21]

By Tuesday morning Washington was saturated with telegrams and newspaper editorials condemning the Selma attack and demanding the passage of voting rights legislation. Fifty congressmen took the House and Senate floors to express outrage; sixty-six signed a telegram to President Johnson urging immediate action. Johnson met with congressional leaders while Vice President Hubert Humphrey met with a delegation representing protest marchers picketing the White House. By afternoon the president had issued a statement deploring the brutality, guaranteeing protection for Alabama marchers, and promising expedited legislation.

On the very night of the attack Dr. King sent out several hundred telegrams: "I call therefore on clergy of all faiths . . . to join me in Selma for a ministers' march to Montgomery on Tuesday morning, March 9th."[22] Governor Wallace vowed to stop a second march.

Federal District Court judge Frank M. Johnson, no friend of Wallace, refused to issue a permit for a second march before holding hearings into the violence at the first one. As more and more eager supporters arrived in Selma, King faced a troubling dilemma. He was loathe to ask the marchers to wait but reluctant to violate the federal injunction. He eventually announced that he would march, and a White House emissary was sent to dissuade him, but King refused to cancel. The president's man met with Lingo and Clark in a used-car lot and crafted a compromise.

King led about two thousand people out of Brown Chapel, including 450 clergymen and women, on the second Selma march. They had been prepared for the worst by Dr. Moldovan:

> Tear gas will *not* keep you from breathing. You may feel like you can't breathe for a while. Tear gas will not make you *permanently* blind. It may make you *temporarily* blind. Do not rub your eyes. . . . If you become unconscious, be sure somebody stays with you." A delighted, outraged laugh rose through the church. The doctor laughed too. "I mean, if you see someone become unconscious, be sure to stay with him." He got the day's greatest ovation.[23]

The march was met, again, by a blockade of troopers. King asked his followers to kneel and pray with him. Instead of charging, the line parted like the Red Sea, leaving the road to Montgomery open. But King could not take that road. Instead, he turned the marchers around and led them back across the bridge. No march down the highway, no attack by the troopers: that was the compromise.

"Turnaround Tuesday," as this march has come to be called, remains an inexplicable moment in civil rights history. When did King agree to this compromise? Why did he tell the marchers that he would lead them all the way? Did he realize that this "betrayal" would quickly deepen the rift developing between the SCLC and SNCC? And how did he feel as his followers sang—both going and coming back—"Ain't Gonna Let Nobody Turn Me 'Round"?

The turnaround left hundreds of green recruits stranded in Selma, in need of food and shelter. Three white Unitarian ministers found themselves dining together Sunday evening at Walker's, a small black soul food restaurant. After dinner they made the mistake of passing the Silver Moon Cafe, a white hangout, where four men jumped out of the shadows and beat them. Rev. James Reeb was clubbed to death.

The tremendous outcry over the killing of the white minister was far louder than that in response to Jimmie Lee Jackson's death—a contrast much noticed in the black community. Senators and congressmen condemned the murder. More telegrams poured into Washington and more editorials proliferated, all calling for voting rights legislation. President Johnson, who was keeping close track of the developments in Selma as his voting rights bill was being drafted, sent Mrs. Reeb yellow roses and flew her home to Boston from her husband's deathbed.

Hundreds of ministers, priests, nuns, and rabbis were heeding King's call to come to Selma. One of them was Father Daniel Berrigan (later prominent in the antiwar movement):

> Monday, March 15. We came in, thirty-five strong, from New York, in time for the memorial service for Reverend Reeb. . . . We approached Brown's Chapel, the reality of Selma hit like a tight fist.
>
> The church was ringed with . . . troopers. They lounged in the open cars, feet hung out of doors and windows, eyes half closed in sunlight; helmets, billy clubs a stereotype of sleepy brutal power. . . .
>
> The church was packed. The TV cameras, the newsmen were there in force, tired out but still there. The nation needed to see this; better, since [Bloody] Sunday, it even wanted to see. A shabby backwater church . . . was for this week the heart and focus of America. In it, the most astounding ironies were being taken for granted. Black store-hands and field workers sat beside distinguished theologians. Hawaiians met New Yorkers, believers shook hands with the unchurched, beatniks sang along with nuns. Men who differed in every conceivable respect—faith and race and culture—found themselves bewildered by a sudden unity whose implications went far beyond the unpredictable days they were enduring together.[24]

SEE PAGE 185

That evening President Johnson presented his voting rights bill to Congress and to television cameras. In what many consider the greatest of all presidential civil rights speeches, Johnson told an audience estimated at seventy million:

> Our fathers believed that if this noble view of the rights of man was to flourish, it must be rooted in democracy. The most basic right of all was the right to choose your own leaders. The history of this country in large measure is the history of the expansion of that right to all of our people. . . .
>
> Wednesday, I will send to Congress a law designed to eliminate illegal barriers to the right to vote. . . .
>
> Even if we pass this bill, the battle will not be over. What happened in Selma is part of a much larger movement that reaches into every section and state of America. It is the effort of American Negroes to secure for themselves the full blessings of American life. Their cause is our cause too. Because it is not just Negroes, but really it is all of us, who must overcome the crippling legacy of bigotry and injustice. And, we shall overcome. . . .
>
> The real hero of this struggle is the American Negro. His actions and protests, his courage to risk safety and even risk his life, have awakened the conscience of this nation. His demonstrations have been designed to call attention to injustice, designed to provoke change, designed to stir reform. He has called upon us to make good the promise of America. And who among us can say that we would have made the same progress if not for his persistent bravery, and faith in democracy.[25]

C. T. Vivian remembered reactions to the speech: "Martin was sitting in a chair looking towards the TV set, and when LBJ said, 'We shall overcome,' we all cheered. I looked over toward Martin and Martin was very quietly sitting in the chair, and a tear ran down his cheek. It was a victory like none other, it was an affirmation of the movement."[26]

On the judicial front, Judge Johnson ruled on Thursday that the third Selma to Montgomery march could proceed and that it must be guaranteed protection. When Governor Wallace refused to commit state forces (citing financial constraints) President Johnson federalized the Alabama National Guard.

The fifty-four-mile Selma to Montgomery march began on Sunday, March 21. Four thousand marchers crossed the Edmund Pettus Bridge and set off down Highway 80, led by Martin Luther King, Jr., Ralph Bunche, Constance Baker Motley, Rabbi Abraham Heschel, and John Lewis, who has recalled:

> It was like a holy crusade, like Gandhi's march to the sea. You didn't get tired, you really didn't get weary, you had to go. It was more than an ordinary march. To me, there was never a march like this one before, and there hasn't been one since. It was the sense of community moving there—as you walked you saw people coming, waving, bringing you food or bringing you something to drink. You saw the power of the most powerful country on the face of the earth, the United States government.[27]

SEE PAGE 182

The march took five days and proceeded without disruption. National Guardsmen —augmented by regular army troops, FBI agents, and U.S. marshals—checked the road for bombs and snipers and kept the hecklers along the route at a distance. Helicopters circled overhead. The tent crew of forty students from San Francisco Theological Seminary pitched the first day's camp about seven miles outside Selma. A hot meal of pork and beans and spaghetti was delivered in eight brand-new galvanized garbage cans; supper was prepared each day by a crew of cooks in the large kitchen of Selma's Green Street Baptist Church.

The Monday-night camp was on the property of a seventy-eight-year-old Lowndes County widow, Rosie Steele. She told a reporter, "I guess I've lived too long and just didn't think things would change—until I heard the President's speech the other night. I knew he was my President too. . . . I almost feel like I might live long enough to vote myself."[28] Tuesday night's campsite was the worst. The land belonged to A. G. Gaston, the black millionaire whose motel had been headquarters for the Birmingham movement. The field had turned to mud in the rain, and no matter how much hay was laid down, many of the marchers could not keep dry.

To keep traffic under control along the two-lane section of the highway, only three hundred marchers were allowed to complete the entire trek. At the edge of Lowndes County the road took on two more lanes and the march reinflated. By the time it left the final campsite, the march comprised over twenty-five thousand people. It was the biggest civil rights gathering the South had ever seen.

The marchers proceeded down Dexter Avenue, Montgomery's main street, and assembled opposite the Dexter Avenue Baptist Church, where the first bus-boycott meetings had been held ten years before. Across the avenue was the Alabama Supreme Court building, where the state ban on the NAACP had been upheld in 1956. Next to the church was the imposing Department of Public Safety building, headquarters of the state troopers. And just past that was the beautiful state capitol. On the portico, set into the top step, was a brass plaque commemorating the inauguration of the first Confederate president in 1861. And it was there that Governor George Wallace had been inaugurated in 1963, vowing, "Segregation today, segregation tomorrow, and segregation forever."

From those steps Martin Luther King, Jr., addressed the rally. He began with Mother Pollard's aphorism, "My feets is tired, but my soul is rested." He recited the history of the civil rights movement, outlined the hard work that lay ahead, then launched into an inspiring oration:

> We must come to see that the end we seek is a society at peace with itself, a society that can live with its conscience. That will be a day not of the white man, not of the black man. That will be the day of man as man.
>
> I know you are asking today, "How long will it take?". . . How long? Not long, because no lie can live forever. How long, not long, because you reap what you sow. How long, not long, because the arc of the moral universe is long but it bends towards justice. . . .
>
> Glory Hallelujah! Glory Hallelujah! Glory Hallelujah! Glory Hallelujah!
> His truth is marching on.[29]

Governor Wallace refused to receive a delegation of marchers. Two weeks later he finally met with a group that included the SCLC's Rev. Joseph Lowery, who recalled:

> He said, "Well, I don't advocate violence." I said, "You don't in so many words, but you do. You get on television, you rave against people taking the rights of little people and the government coming in and stirring up trouble, and you get your emotions released on TV. But the fella in the dark street, he doesn't have that forum, so he gets a lead pipe to identify with you, and cracks somebody's skull. . . ."
>
> We moralized his conscience that day, I think. . . .
>
> He probably for the first time got to see face to face how the black community felt about him and his leadership.[30]

The Voting Rights Act of 1965 became law on August 6. It had the strong provisions for federal registrars and against voter examinations that civil rights advocates had demanded. Within a year there were about nine thousand new black registrants in Dallas County. In the next election, they provided Wilson Baker with the margin needed to replace Jim Clark as sheriff. The number of black voters registered to vote leaped from an estimated

23 percent of voting-age blacks in this country in 1964 to 61 percent in 1969. In Mississippi the increase in the same period was from 6.7 percent to 66.5 percent.[31] Southern politics was radically changed. Eight-year-old marcher Sheyann Webb remembered:

SEE PAGE 187

> I felt real good at the last march. It was like we *had* overcome. We had reached the point we were fighting for, for a long time. And if you were to just stand there in the midst of thousands and thousands of people and all the great leaders and political people who had come from all over the world, it was just a thrill.
>
> I asked my mother and father for my birthday present to become registered voters. They took me to the polls with them to vote.[32]

A CARICATURE OF SHERIFF JIM CLARK AND A
DRAWING OF MARTIN LUTHER KING, JR., POSTED ON
A WALL, SELMA, ALABAMA, 1965. **DECLAN HAUN**

A CONFRONTATION BETWEEN REV. C. T. VIVIAN AND
SHERIFF JIM CLARK, SELMA, FEBRUARY 5, 1965.
HORACE CORT

"A PRAYER AT THE COURTHOUSE—C. T. Vivian, Negro
integration leader, leads a prayer on the courthouse steps in
Selma, Ala. today after Sheriff James Clark, rear, stopped
him at the door with a court order. Vivian led hundreds of
demonstrators armed with petitions asking longer voter registration hours. Clark arrested them when they refused to
disperse." (Original AP caption.)

BELOW: MEMBERS OF SHERIFF CLARK'S POSSE PREPARE
TO CONFRONT THE FIRST SELMA MARCH, MARCH 7, 1965.
CHARLES MOORE

OPPOSITE: ANDREW YOUNG LEADS MARCHERS IN
PRAYER OUTSIDE BROWN CHAPEL JUST BEFORE THEY
SET OFF ON THE FIRST SELMA MARCH, MARCH 7, 1965.
SPIDER MARTIN

Andrew Young was a senior SCLC director and a close confidant of Martin Luther King, Jr. To Young's right is Hosea Williams of the SCLC; next to Williams (in the white coat) is John Lewis, SNCC's chairman. On Young's left is SNCC's Lafayette Surney; next to Surney is Amelia Boynton (with bowed head), a longtime Selma voting-rights advocate.

Just after this prayer 600 marchers left Brown Chapel, headed for the Edmund Pettus Bridge and Montgomery.

TROOPERS CHARGING MARCHERS AT THE
PETTUS BRIDGE. **SPIDER MARTIN**

At the center John Lewis is receiving the beating that
would send him to the hospital for three days.

CONFRONTATION AT THE PETTUS BRIDGE,
MARCH 7, 1965. **SPIDER MARTIN**

The troopers are advancing, gas masks on, with Major
John Cloud in the lead. At the head of the march are (left to
right): Hosea Williams, John Lewis, Marion activist Albert
Turner, SNCC's Bob Mants, and Jerry Harrison of Selma.

BELOW: STATE TROOPER STANDING OVER AMELIA
BOYNTON, MARCH 7, 1965. **SPIDER MARTIN**

RIGHT: TWO YOUNG MARCHERS LIFTING THE WOUNDED
AMELIA BOYNTON. **SPIDER MARTIN**

Mrs. Boynton later recalled:

> I felt a blow on my arm that could have injured me perma-
> nently had it been on my head. Another blow by a trooper
> as I was gasping for breath knocked me to the ground and
> there I lay unconscious. Others told me that my attacker
> had called to another that he had "the damn leader." One
> of them shot tear gas all over me. The plastic rain cap that
> Margaret Moore gave me may have saved my life; it had
> slipped down over my face and protected my nose some-
> what from the worst of the fumes. Pictures in the paper and
> those in the possession of the Justice Department show
> the trooper standing over me with a club. Some of the
> marchers said to the trooper, "She is dead." And they were
> told to drag me to the side of the road.

JUNIATA COLLEGE STUDENT PAM CLEMSON HELPS A
BEATEN FELLOW DEMONSTRATOR, MONTGOMERY,
MARCH 16, 1965. **CHARLES MOORE**

On March 16, the day after President Johnson declared
"We shall overcome" in his major civil rights speech,
SNCC's executive secretary James Forman organized a student protest in Montgomery in support of the Selma
marchers. Before they could assemble, the students were
attacked by a club-wielding posse on horseback; many
were injured and arrested. At a rally later that day Forman
proclaimed in rage, "If we can't sit at the table of democracy, then we'll knock the fucking legs off."

Pam Clemson called herself "seventeen-years-old and
out to save the world." She was arrested after this scene
and spent several days in jail.

THE SELMA TO MONTGOMERY MARCH, MARCH 21–25, 1965. **JAMES KARALES**

James Karales's stirring images of the Selma to Montgomery march were commissioned for a *Look* magazine story called "Turning Point for the Church," which highlighted the moral awakening of the northern white clergy. Karales was accompanied by the reporter Christopher Wren, who wrote about the marchers:

> Sustained by rationed peanut-butter sandwiches, they never faltered in their pace and bitter humor. "I've been called nigger," said somebody up front. "Well, from now on, it's got to be "Mister Nigger." Across the Black Belt farmland rolled the pickup words of their new battle hymn: "Oh, Wallace, you know you can't jail us all; Oh Wallace, segregation's bound to fall." In it, the white ministers, priests, rabbis, and nuns, who had jetted vast distances to reinforce the march, found a new statement of faith.

BELOW: JAMES FORMAN AND JAMES BALDWIN ON THE
SELMA TO MONTGOMERY MARCH. **STEVE SCHAPIRO**

ABOVE: THE SELMA TO MONTGOMERY MARCH.
JAMES KARALES

OPPOSITE, TOP: WATCHING THE SELMA TO
MONTGOMERY MARCH. **BILL STRODE**

OPPOSITE, BOTTOM: NUNS ON THE SELMA TO
MONTGOMERY MARCH. **STEVE SCHAPIRO**

"I went South," said Father Dom Orsini, "not realizing I would study the North when I was there. I saw in Selma what I had never realized was also in Pittsburgh. Our discrimination is just more sophisticated up here."

OPPOSITE: THE SELMA TO MONTGOMERY MARCH.
SPIDER MARTIN

ABOVE: THE SELMA TO MONTGOMERY MARCH.
BRUCE DAVIDSON

One marcher inscribed his message in the sunscreen on his forehead. The young man with the flag is also shown on page 163.

THE RALLY AT THE END OF THE SELMA
TO MONTGOMERY MARCH, MARCH 25,
1965. **BRUCE DAVIDSON**

LEFT: VIOLA LIUZZO. **UNITED PRESS INTERNATIONAL**

BELOW: THE CAR OF VIOLA LIUZZO, A CIVIL RIGHTS WORKER MURDERED AT THE END OF THE SELMA TO MONTGOMERY MARCH, LOWNDES COUNTY, MARCH 25, 1965. **BRUCE DAVIDSON**

Viola Liuzzo, who had driven down from her home in Detroit to join the march, was murdered in her car by four Klansmen on a road between Selma and Montgomery. Four days after the shooting J. Edgar Hoover went on television to announce the apprehension of four suspects. One of the four, Gary Thomas Rowe, a devoted Klansman who relished violence, was also an FBI informant. A jury ignored Rowe's testimony in acquitting Klansman Collie Leroy Wilkins of the murder.

TENT CITY, GREENE COUNTY, ALABAMA, MAY 4, 1966.
CHARMIAN READING

Reading recalls:

This seventeen-year-old woman posed for me with her mother and younger cousin in their tent. They were one of several families evicted from a plantation because they had registered to vote; they lived in tents on a friend's farm. I was in Greene County with Phyllis Cunningham of the Medical Committee for Human Rights, trying to deal with some of the health problems there.

Four days after this picture was taken, the young woman went into labor. The local white hospital turned her away; on the drive to another hospital, she bled to death.

8

BLACK POWER AND THE MARCH AGAINST FEAR, 1966
"The Oppressed Against the Oppressor"

In early 1964 SNCC chairman John Lewis told *Dialogue* magazine: "Something is happening to people in the Southern Negro community. They're identifying with people because of color. . . . They're conscious of things that happen in Cuba, in Latin America, and in Africa. . . . There's been a radical change in our people since 1960; the way they dress, the music they listen to, their natural hairdos—all of them want to go to Africa. . . . I think people are searching for a sense of identity, and they're finding it."[1]

Later that year Lewis crossed paths with Malcolm X at the New Stanley Hotel in Nairobi, Kenya. Lewis was with a SNCC tour group that included Fannie Lou Hamer, Julian Bond, James Forman, Robert Moses, and Harry Belafonte (SNCC's major financial supporter). Belafonte had organized the tour to help the members recover from the violence of Freedom Summer and from the betrayal of the MFDP at the Democratic convention. He also wanted the SNCC members to get to know Africa and to meet some new African leaders. Lewis recalled his Kenya conversations with Malcolm X:

> While we were meeting in a little coffee shop at the hotel, he said, "Always sit with your back to the wall, so you can look out and see who is watching you." He told us to be careful . . . he kept saying over and over again that he really wanted to be helpful and be supportive of the civil rights movement. And he wanted to visit the South.
>
> He also told us over and over again to keep fighting. "Don't give up," he said. "This is an ongoing struggle. Be prepared for the worst, but keep it up, keep fighting. People are changing, there are people supporting you all over the world."[2]

At SNCC's invitation, Malcolm X traveled to Selma on February 4, 1965. He told several hundred protesters at Brown Chapel to put American racism on trial before the world by taking their demands not only to President Johnson but also to the United Nations. After Malcolm X, Coretta Scott King spoke. Then Malcolm told her: "Mrs. King, will you tell Dr. King that I planned to visit with him in jail? I won't get a chance now because I've got to leave to get to New York in time to catch a plane to London where I'm to address the African Students' Conference. I want Dr. King to know that I didn't come to Selma to make his job difficult. I really did come thinking that I could make it easier. If the white people realize what the alternative is, perhaps they will be more willing to hear Dr. King."[3]

SEE PAGE 200

Malcolm X, who had earlier been notoriously caustic about the strategies of the civil rights movement, was showing more respect for certain movement initiatives. And SNCC activists were paying more heed to Malcolm X, to his calls for black self-sufficiency and for linking African-American struggles to the worldwide anticolonial struggle—"a global rebellion of the oppressed against the oppressor, the exploited against the exploiter."[4] But this new dialogue came to an abrupt end. Three weeks after his visit to Selma, Malcolm X was assassinated by Black Muslim hitmen in the Audubon Ballroom in Harlem.

Malcolm X was not a part of the civil rights movement that was founded on non-violent resistance, but his message became an increasingly important complement to it. Malcolm X gave voice, more loudly than ever before, to black rage. By standing apart in fearless rejection of white society, he personified black pride. Julius Lester has written vividly about his importance: "More than any other person, Malcolm X was responsible for the growing consciousness and new militancy of black people. . . . His clear uncomplicated words cut through the chains on black minds like a giant blowtorch. . . . He was not concerned with stirring the moral conscience of America, because he knew— America has no moral conscience."[5]

In 1965 Lowndes County, Alabama, which straddled the route of the Selma to Montgomery march, was one of the poorest counties in the nation. Out of a population of fifteen thousand, twelve thousand were black. Not one was registered to vote. Ninety white families owned 90 percent of the land. As the march passed through the county, SNCC's Stokely Carmichael talked with the local blacks who had stayed on the sidelines, wrote down their names, and promised to return to help organize them.

The next day he did return and set to work. When the Voting Rights Act became law in August 1965, Lowndes County was one of the first areas to get a federal registrar to enforce the new law. Blacks registered by the hundreds, and they thought hard about how to use their votes. Supporting the Democratic Party seemed pointless; the chairman of the

Lowndes County Democratic Committee stood accused, in a federal suit, of evicting black tenant farmers who had registered. An obscure Alabama law was discovered that enabled the ready formation of a new county party—the Lowndes County Freedom Organization. Organized by Carmichael and others, the LCFO came to be called the Black Panther party because of the insignia they adopted. The symbol of the regular Democratic Party in Alabama was a strutting white rooster emblazoned with the words "White Supremacy for the Right." What better to thrash a white cock than a leaping black panther? The LCFO's militant electoral efforts generated violent white opposition—Jonathan Daniels, a white seminary student helping the effort, was shot to death. Though they won no seats, the LCFO had proven that they could successfully run candidates in both primary and general county elections.

The Black Panther Party's success in Lowndes County inspired the formation of similar grassroots black political organizations around the nation, some of which would adopt the panther name and symbol. As the Black Panther Party was gearing up for the election in Lowndes County, Bobby Seale and Huey Newton founded the Black Panther Party for Self-Defense in Oakland, California. Newton said: "Our program was structured after the Black Muslim program—minus the religion. I was very impressed with Malcolm X, with the program that Malcolm X followed. I think that I became disillusioned with the Muslims after Malcolm X was assassinated. I think that I was following not Elijah Muhammad or the Muslims, but Malcolm X himself." Seale added: "We flipped a coin to see who would be chairman. I won chairman. . . . Huey and I began to try to figure out how we could organize youthful black folks into some kind of political, electoral, power movement. Stokely Carmichael was on the scene with Black Power."[6]

The phrase "Black Power" first caught the attention of the media during the Meredith march. Lester described the march's beginning:

SEE PAGE 215

> In June of 1966, James Meredith, the first Negro to graduate from the University of Mississippi, began what he called a "March against Fear" through his native state. He said that he wanted "to tear down the fear that grips the Negroes in Mississippi and . . . encourage the 450,000 [to register to vote] in Mississippi."
>
> With this announcement black people across the country began crossing Meredith's name from the list of those in the land of the living. Hustlers began checking whether they could take out insurance policies on his life, naming themselves as beneficiaries. Ministers looked through their files, searching for old sermons about martyrdom. In a few places florists hurriedly placed orders for funeral wreaths, to be sure they would have enough on hand. They weren't being cynical. They were black and they knew. Mr. Meredith had announced his death.[7]

On the second morning of his projected 220-mile march from Memphis to Jackson,

Meredith was felled by two shotgun blasts from a sniper—a forty-year-old Klansman who had been waiting in ambush. Although initial wire-service reports and photographs indicated that Meredith had been killed, he recovered in the hospital quickly enough to rejoin the march later. As word of the shooting spread, the major civil rights leaders rushed to Meredith's bedside and vowed to march on. Martin Luther King, Jr., of the SCLC, Whitney Young, Jr., of the National Urban League, and the NAACP's Roy Wilkins came down, as did Floyd McKissick, CORE's new leader. McKissick, who had been so important in organizing the 1960 sit-ins in Durham, North Carolina, had just replaced James Farmer at the head of CORE. McKissick's militancy made him a controversial choice, and his accession signaled both the group's growing black nationalism and its increasing skepticism about previous methods. McKissick called nonviolence "a dying philosophy" that had "outlived its usefulness."[8]

Stokely Carmichael joined the march as SNCC's new chair, having just defeated John Lewis in a bitter fight. Carmichael's election, like McKissick's, was seen as a repudiation of nonviolence. As Carmichael remembered:

> The SNCC people had seen raw terror and they understood properly this terror had nothing to do with morality but had to do clearly with power. It was a question of economic power, of the exploitation of our people. . . . We saw the political organization of the masses as the only route to solving our problem. We placed a strong emphasis on the fact that nonviolence for us was a tactic and not a philosophy, as it was for the SCLC. Our direction was clear, with a heavy emphasis on nationalism. And strong, as strong as Malcolm had it, as strong as we could get it.[9]

The march worked its way down the length of Mississippi, boiling with tensions between the factions. One argument raged over the arrival of the Deacons of Defense and Justice—an armed self-defense group based in Bogalusa, Louisiana. After McKissick and Carmichael argued that they should be allowed to protect the marchers, King reluctantly agreed to their inclusion but Young and Wilkins left the march in protest.

The March Against Fear was also a mobile voter-registration campaign, with canvassers going off into surrounding counties to encourage enrollment. Over four thousand black voters were registered.

Evenings were occasions for speeches in which King, McKissick, and Carmichael competed for the hearts of Mississippi—and national—audiences. As the march entered the Delta region, SNCC organizer Willie Ricks began to lace his speeches with the slogan "Black Power!" Ricks reported back to incredulous fellow SNCC workers about the tremendous impact of the phrase, how audiences would brazenly pick up the shout and not let it go. Chairman Carmichael told Cleveland Sellers, "You know, you sent the wrong man out because we need a clear analysis here and this man is given to exaggerations

SEE PAGE 213

and talking all sorts of nonsense in hyperbolic terms." But after Carmichael went out to watch Ricks in action, he came to appreciate the power of "Black Power."[10] The phrase had long been around, having been used by Ralph Ellison, Adam Clayton Powell, Jr., and Paul Robeson without much notice. Now it was becoming a rallying cry—one with many meanings—that was competing with "Freedom Now!"

It was Carmichael's speech in Greenwood on the evening of June 16 that began to popularize "Black Power." Greenwood had been the major SNCC stronghold in the Mississippi Delta since 1962. Carmichael had been arrested there several times; in fact, he was jailed again on the day of the speech, then bailed out. Carmichael stood before an audience of six hundred, the last to speak after McKissick, King, and Ricks. He spoke with anger about his many arrests and about the many years of struggle for minimal results. He concluded: "What we gonna start saying now is 'black power.'" He set up a call that had the audience shouting back with excitement: "We want—Black Power! We want—Black Power! What do we want? Black Power! What do we want? Black Power! We want—Black Power!"[11]

SEE PAGE 212

The national news media were quick to portray the new slogan as a major turning point in the civil rights movement—and to condemn it. Critics willfully confused "power" with violence. McKissick and Carmichael defended the phrase as a just demand for no more than what other groups had in America. Carmichael talked about black power as black electoral power and about the need to "build a power base . . . so strong that we will bring [whites] to their knees every time they mess with us."[12] King recognized the appeal of the idea and the rage that lay behind the enthusiastic response to it. But he was afraid that the phrase would alienate white supporters, would be used to justify white backlash, and would discourage nonviolent protest. He told a reporter: "Because Stokely Carmichael chose the March as an arena for a debate over black power, we didn't get to emphasize the evils of Mississippi and the need for the 1966 Civil Rights Act. Internal dissension along the March helped Mississippi get off the hook somewhat."[13]

On June 22 King and other marchers made a detour to Philadelphia, Mississippi, to commemorate Chaney, Goodman, and Schwerner, who had been murdered near there two years before. King was confronted at the courthouse by Chief Deputy Sheriff Cecil Price. King asked, "You're the fellow that had Schwerner and those fellows in jail?" "Yes, sir," Price drawled. As King led a brief memorial service, he was heckled by a vicious white mob. "I believe in my heart that the murderers are somewhere around me at this moment," King said. From the rear he heard Price reply, "You're damn right, they're right behind you right now." King would later say that as he stood there he "yielded to the real possibility of the inevitability of death." As the service ended, the marchers were attacked by the mob, as were the camera crews filming the events.[14]

Two days later the marchers were brutally clubbed and teargassed by state police in Canton. It was an attack almost as devastating as the one that had ended the first

Selma march, but it received scant media or political attention. The final rally in Jackson on June 26, which attracted about fifteen thousand people, was a relatively despondent affair, dampened by the relentless Mississippi hostility and the increasing divisions within the movement itself. Nonetheless, Floyd McKissick declared presciently: "1966 shall be remembered as the year we left our imposed status as Negroes and became *Black Men*. . . . 1966 is the year of the concept of Black Power."[15] Meredith commented on the March Against Fear that he had started: "If Negroes ever do overcome fear, the white man has only two choices: to kill them or let them be free."[16]

MALCOLM X AT A JOB DISCRIMINATION PROTEST, BROOKLYN, JULY/AUGUST 1963. **BOB ADELMAN**

Brooklyn CORE, along with the NAACP and a coalition of black Brooklyn ministers, organized thousands of demonstrators for three weeks of picketing for black jobs at the construction site of Downtown Medical Center. By July 30 over six hundred demonstrators had been arrested. There were numerous complaints of police brutality.

Malcolm X, who was greatly admired by Brooklyn CORE chairman Olly Leeds and by many other CORE members, turned out for one demonstration. He is carrying a copy of the Nation of Islam newspaper *Muhammad Speaks*. The full headline read, "URGE NEGROES TO UNITE: Harlem in Unity Rally."

MALCOLM X ADDRESSING A HARLEM RALLY, MAY 14, 1963.
UNITED PRESS INTERNATIONAL

"Black Muslim leader Malcolm X has assistant hold a picture of fallen black men as he addresses a Harlem rally in support of integration efforts in Birmingham, Ala. late May 14th. (The picture held was taken in Los Angeles, 4/27/62, after a riot erupted in front of the local headquarters of the extremist Black Muslim sect.) Later, as the two-hour rally was breaking up, violence erupted among the crowd of spectators. At least two store windows were broken, and police reinforcements were called in to restore order." (Original UPI caption.)

The "New Theresa" sign is for the Hotel Theresa, where Malcolm X sometimes stayed.

MALCOLM X AND CASSIUS CLAY/MUHAMMAD ALI
CLOWNING IN A MIAMI RESTAURANT AFTER CLAY/ALI'S
HEAVYWEIGHT VICTORY, FEBRUARY 26, 1964.
BOB GOMEL

By the end of February 1964, Malcolm X had been suspended from the Nation of Islam. A few days later he joined
his friend Cassius Clay in Florida and was present when Clay
knocked out Sonny Liston to become heavyweight champion
of the world. Clay had secretly been a member of the Nation
since 1961. The day after winning the title, he announced
his conversion and his new name, Muhammad Ali.

LEFT: MALCOLM X AND MARTIN LUTHER KING, JR., CAPITOL HILL, WASHINGTON, D.C., MARCH 26, 1964. **ASSOCIATED PRESS**

King and Malcolm X met only once, by chance. King was at the Capitol for a meeting with liberal senators Hubert Humphrey, Thomas Kuchel, Philip Hart, Paul Douglas, and Jacob Javits; he was seeking support for the civil rights bill, which segregationist senators were filibustering. King told reporters that he was contemplating a direct-action campaign in Washington.

In the summer of 1960 Malcolm X had written to King to challenge his position against racial separatism and to invite him to attend an Elijah Muhammad appearance. King wrote back cordially declining the invitation; his letter was headed "Dear Mr. X."

OPPOSITE: CONTACT SHEET SHOWING MALCOLM X, CORETTA SCOTT KING, AND OTHERS ADDRESSING A MEETING AT BROWN CHAPEL, SELMA, FEBRUARY 4, 1965. **FRANCIS MITCHELL**

Top row: Juanita Abernathy, Malcolm X, Malcolm X and Coretta Scott King; second row: Fred Shuttlesworth, Andrew Young and James Bevel, Malcolm X and King; third row: Malcolm X, audience; fourth row: King, Abernathy; fifth row: audience, King; sixth row: Malcolm X, seventh row: Shuttlesworth.

Francis Mitchell, a photojournalist and writer who worked for *Jet* and *Ebony* magazines and later for SNCC, remembers: "Malcolm drove up from Tuskegee in a fancy Jag or something. We sent someone to tell Malcolm that we hoped he would observe the protocol, that there would be no talk of violence. He proceeded to say what he wanted to say."

MALCOLM X ARRIVING AT HIS HOUSE IN EAST ELMHURST, QUEENS, AFTER IT WAS FIREBOMBED, FEBRUARY 14, 1965. **UNITED PRESS INTERNATIONAL**

Gene Roberts, a New York police officer who had infiltrated Malcolm X's Organization of Afro-American Unity, recalls: "When Malcolm's house was fire-bombed, there were a lot of rumors. The police department did it, the FBI-CIA did it, Elijah's people. But everybody agreed to the fact that he was in mortal danger."

MALCOLM X, SHOT TO DEATH, BEING RUSHED FROM THE
AUDUBON BALLROOM, HARLEM, FEBRUARY 21, 1965.
UNITED PRESS INTERNATIONAL

Three Muslims were convicted of Malcolm X's murder, but it
is still not known who ordered the assassination.

OPPOSITE: MEMBERS OF THE MUSLIM WOMEN'S CORPS, SAVIOR'S DAY, CHICAGO, 1967. **ROBERT SENGSTACKE**

RIGHT: THE MARCH AGAINST FEAR, MISSISSIPPI, JUNE 6–26, 1966. **MARIA VARELA**

Maria Varela—along with Casey Hayden, Robert Zellner, and others—worked concurrently for the Students for a Democratic Society (SDS) and SNCC. In 1963 Varela established a SNCC adult-literacy project in Selma. Varela, Hayden, Mary King, and Bob Fletcher set up a SNCC darkroom near Tougaloo College in Jackson, Mississippi, in 1964 or '65.

BELOW: JAMES MEREDITH ON HIS MARCH AGAINST
FEAR, HERNANDO, MISSISSIPPI, JUNE 6, 1966.
VERNON MERRITT III

OPPOSITE: JAMES MEREDITH WOUNDED DURING HIS
MARCH AGAINST FEAR, HERNANDO, JUNE 6, 1966.
VERNON MERRITT III

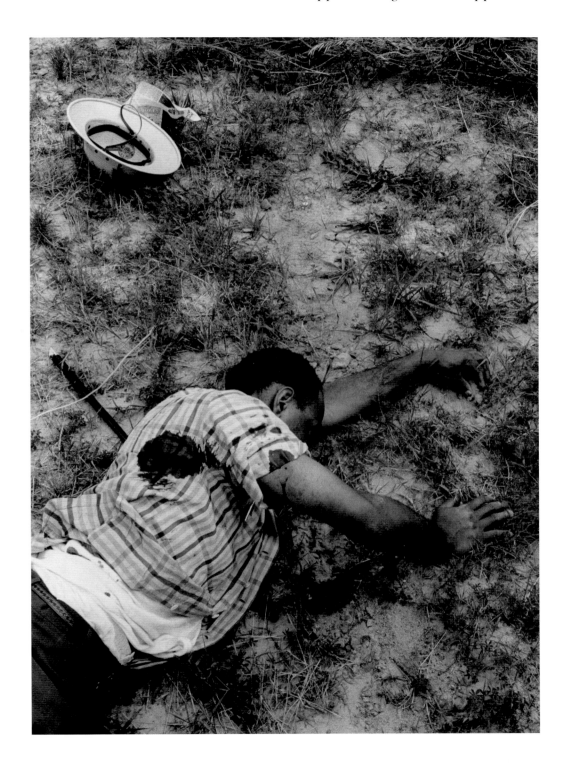

FANNIE LOU HAMER SINGING AT A RALLY DURING THE
MARCH AGAINST FEAR, ENID DAM, YALOBUSHA COUNTY,
MISSISSIPPI, JUNE 12, 1966. **CHARMIAN READING**

A BLIND MAN AND HIS WIFE BEING HELPED ACROSS THE
ROAD TO THE VOTER REGISTRATION OFFICE BY WILLIE
BLUE OF SNCC, CHARLESTON, MISSISSIPPI, JUNE 13, 1966.
CHARMIAN READING

Reading recalls:

After breakfast we drove from the Enid Dam campsite into Yalobusha County to do voter registration. We saw pick-up trucks with rifles, so we stopped and segregated the cars to be less noticeable. We scouted Charleston, which had one long street. At one end was the Post Office, a Federal building that held the voter registration office, and at the other end was the black-owned Foxes' Funeral Home, where we agreed to meet after splitting up to look for people to register.

Word got out about our canvassing, and pick-up trucks and cars began collecting in town. The large plate-glass window at Foxes' seemed too dangerous, so we moved to the Friendly Cafe next door, a nice dark place without windows. During lunch we were told that Willie Blue was going to bring an old couple by car to meet us at the Post Office. We walked two by two down the shaded side of the street; it felt like a gauntlet, with the pick-up trucks driving slowly beside us. I wondered what I was doing away from my four little girls at home, and tried concentrating on camera mechanics to block my fear. With my camera I wasn't allowed inside the registration office, where it would have felt much safer.

Willie Blue drove up at last with a blind man and his wife. Blue worked for SNCC in Chicago, but was from the Charleston area, where his mother still worked on a plantation. He said it was his first time organizing back home. He helped the couple into the Post Office to register. After twenty minutes, they came out. We congratulated the old people as they got back in the car to be driven home. Then we had the long walk through the Mississippi shadows back to the Friendly Cafe.

SNCC CHAIRMAN STOKELY CARMICHAEL CALLING FOR
"BLACK POWER," GREENWOOD, MISSISSIPPI, JUNE 16,
1966. **BOB FITCH**

LEADERS OF THE MARCH AGAINST FEAR ATTEMPTING TO
SET UP A TENT, CANTON, MISSISSIPPI, JUNE 24, 1966.
MATT HERRON

From left to right: Unidentified marcher, Stokely Carmichael, Willie Ricks (in sunglasses), Floyd McKissick, Martin Luther King, Jr.

Near the end of the three-week march, a campsite was planned for the yard of a black public-school yard in Canton. Town officials refused permission. A standoff between about twenty-five-hundred march supporters and a heavily armed contingent of state troopers ended at 8:40 P.M., when the troopers rioted. They fired volley after volley of teargas grenades, then "they came stomping in, behind the gas, gun-butting and kicking the men, women, and children. They were not arresting, they were punishing," recorded journalist Paul Good. A Canton resident working with the Child Development Group of Mississippi witnessed a young woman tackle her mother to the ground: "She screamed, 'Mama, crawl, crawl, don't rub your eyes, Mama, crawl.' She couldn't crawl. It had bursted into her eyes. She was overcome. She just lay in the field on her face. She thought she was dying. The skin on her face was all burned off." Dr. Alvin Poussaint, who was on the march with the Medical Committee for Human Rights, remembers, "We were up that whole night treating the victims."

LEFT: TEAR-GASSED MARCHERS, CANTON, MISSISSIPPI, JUNE 24, 1966. **MATT HERRON**

OPPOSITE: ELDRIDGE AND KATHLEEN CLEAVER, ALGIERS, 1970. **GORDON PARKS**

When this picture was made, Eldridge Cleaver was head of the International Section of the Black Panther Party and was living abroad in exile. Kathleen Cleaver, a former SNCC member, was also an important Black Panther leader. Pictured above them is the Party founder Huey Newton.

Gordon Parks, who covered the Black Panthers for *Life,* remembers telling one young party member:

"I'm in the fight the same as you are. I ride with you every night. You have chosen a gun; I have chosen a camera. I know there is a policeman following us. Every night we are trailed. They are waiting to shoot us up. Do you think their bullets are going to miss me and go to you because I'm Gordon Parks? I'm taking risks to show that you might have a voice. Because so far, nobody in the big press is listening to what you have to say. But here and now *Life* magazine is riding with you. I'm risking my life just being with you. So, my weapon's here with me; your weapon is in your pocket. You've got a 45 in your pocket. But I think my weapon is stronger." And it proved to be. The kid got killed three months later in a shootout. Eldridge Cleaver asked me to become the Panther's information specialist.

9

THE ECLIPSING OF NONVIOLENCE, 1965–68
"It Is Not Over"

In August 1965, just days after the Voting Rights Act was signed into law, an act of police brutality sparked a violent uprising in the Watts ghetto in southwest Los Angeles. The next six days saw the most violent racial rebellion in U.S. history. Enraged residents threw Molotov cocktails and looted and burned white-owned stores. Fourteen thousand National Guardsmen were sent in to control the rioting. Thirty-four people were killed (thirty-one of them black), one thousand were seriously injured, and four thousand were jailed.

Martin Luther King, Jr., flew into Los Angeles in the midst of the riots. Bayard Rustin recalled that King "was absolutely undone" by his tour of Watts and became more conscious than ever that the economic problems of the black underclass constituted the movement's toughest challenge. King told reporters that Watts was "a class revolt of underprivileged against privileged."[1] He met with the mayor, the police chief, and the governor, all of whom angrily dismissed his pleas that they do something about the underlying causes of the rioting.

The summer of 1966 disillusioned and exhausted King. Riots broke out in over twenty ghettos across the nation. "Black power" was dividing the movement and fueling white backlash. Republican congressmen torpedoed the latest federal civil rights bill because they opposed its fair-housing clause. The SCLC's ambitious Summer Community Organization and Political Education program (SCOPE), an attempt to repeat the Mississippi Summer Project across several southern states, was in financial and administrative disarray. "The decade of 1955 to 1965, with its constructive elements, misled us," King would say. "Everyone underestimated the amount of rage Negroes were suppressing, and the amount of bigotry the white majority was disguising."[2]

As King and the movement were formulating new initiatives, white America was becoming more obdurate. Media coverage of the "long, hot summers" destroyed much of the goodwill that the civil rights movement had accumulated. Shallow sympathies evaporated when "the image of the Negro . . . was no longer that of the praying, long-suffering nonviolent victim of Southern sheriffs; it was of a defiant young hoodlum shouting 'black power' and hurling 'Molotov cocktails' in an urban slum."[3] As one study reported, "Television thus aided passage of civil rights legislation, but also permitted the rapid mobilization of adverse white reactions to Negro violence in the wake of the Watts riots."[4]

King said, "Since the riots we just feel that there is a need to kind of reevaluate our whole programmatic thrust . . . particularly re our work in the North. Because Chicago has been pleading with us to come in."[5] Chicago's Coordinating Council of Community Organizations asked the SCLC to join with them in the Chicago Freedom Movement. The SCLC, after forceful debate, accepted the offer, recognizing that Chicago had aspects that could make it the Birmingham or Selma of the North. The nation's second largest city, Chicago housed 800,000 African Americans—a number that had increased 300,000 in a decade—almost all of whom were squeezed into overcrowded, poorly serviced ghettos. It was "the most residentially segregated large city in the nation," according to the 1959 U.S. Commission on Civil Rights. Chicago had strong civil rights organizations that had coordinated a school boycott in 1962 to protest school segregation. It had an entrenched Democratic machine run by Mayor Richard Daley that had the power to change the city—if forced to do so. As King put it, "Chicago . . . could well become the metropolis where a meaningful nonviolent movement could arouse the conscience of this nation to deal with the northern ghetto."[6]

On July 10, 1966, just two weeks after the end of the Meredith march, King led a march of 30,000–60,000 protesters (the number varied according to who did the estimating) on Chicago's city hall. The demands included black jobs, an end to discrimination by realtors, desegregation of public schools, and the establishment of a civilian review board to control police brutality. King's speech to the rally incorporated some of the new "black power" concepts: "We must appreciate our great heritage. We must be proud of our race. We must not be ashamed of being black. We must believe with all of our hearts that black is as beautiful as any other color."[7] Mayor Daley reacted angrily to the demands, claiming that Chicago already had a "massive" antislum program.

Two days later, in oppressive mid-ninety-degree heat, there began clashes between black residents and police that went on for several days, leaving two dead and sixty-five injured. While Mayor Daley was blaming outside agitators, including King, for the riots,

King gathered leaders of the major youth gangs—the Cobras, the Vice Lords, and the Roman Saints—to his apartment and persuaded them to forswear further attacks.

But new violence erupted when Jesse Jackson, Al Raby, and others in the Chicago Freedom Movement led small marches through the all-white neighborhoods of Gage Park, Marquette Park, and Cicero—home to first- and second-generation European immigrants. Mobs followed the marchers. They sported "white power" symbols, they cursed and taunted, they threw rocks, bottles, bricks, and cherry bombs. Police escorts offered only feeble protection, and hundreds of marchers were injured. Andrew Young remembered "a rough day where maybe a couple of hundred demonstrators were surrounded by a mob of ten thousand or more. Now, in the South we faced mobs, but it would be a couple of hundred or even fifty, or seventy-five. The violence in the South always came from a rabble element. But these were women and children and husbands and wives coming out of their homes becoming a mob—and in some ways it was more frightening."[8] King said, "I have never seen—even in Mississippi and Alabama—mobs as hostile and hate-filled as I've seen in Chicago."[9]

Embarrassed by the national attention given to the "White Power" attacks, Daley sponsored negotiating sessions between the civil rights leaders, realty representatives, and politicians. In the midst of these meetings he also maneuvered a double-dealing court injunction against further marching. Still, an accord was finally reached that gave the movement some of the concessions it had been seeking—at least on paper. King called it the "most significant and far reaching victory that has ever come about in a northern community on the whole question of open housing."[10] But the agreement was immediately criticized within the movement as getting too little too soon, and in fact it did not actually integrate the city's housing. King received a lot of the blame for the Chicago debacle, which proved to many that nonviolent tactics were of little use in the North.

By 1967 Bayard Rustin and other theoreticians were advising the civil rights movement to move "from protest to politics" by establishing strong political alliances and constituencies. But King was moving from social reform to social revolution:

> If we look honestly at the realities of our national life it is clear that we are not marching forward, we are groping and stumbling. We are divided and confused. Our moral values and our spiritual confidence sink even as our material wealth ascends. In these trying circumstances the black revolution is much more than a struggle for the rights of Negroes. It is, rather, forcing America to face all its interrelated flaws: racism, poverty, militarism, and materialism. It is exposing evils that are rooted deeply in the whole structure of our society. It reveals systematic rather than superficial flaws, and it suggests that radical reconstruction of society itself is the real issue to be faced.[11]

King took a stand that reaffirmed his basic creed of nonviolence and that alienated him from powerful allies and the majority of the American public. Since early 1965 he

SEE PAGE 227

had frequently denounced American involvement in the Vietnam War. On April 4, 1967, in New York's Riverside Church, King came out with full force against the war:

> This business of burning human beings with napalm, of filling our nation's homes with orphans and widows, of injecting poisonous drugs into the veins of peoples normally humane, of sending men home from dark and bloody battlefields physically handicapped and psychologically deranged, cannot be reconciled with wisdom, justice and love. A nation that continues year after year to spend more money on military defense than on programs of social uplift is approaching spiritual death.[12]

Carl Rowan, the black reporter whose help had been so providential during the Montgomery bus boycott, was a columnist at the *Washington Post* in 1967 and one of the first to criticize King's speech: "Many who have listened to him with respect will never accord him the same confidence. He has diminished his usefulness to his cause, to his country, and to his people."[13] The NAACP board of directors voted to censure any merging of the civil rights and antiwar movements. *Life* called the speech "a demagogic slander that sounded like a speech for Radio Hanoi." FBI director Hoover used the speech to intensify his slanderous attacks on King, writing to President Johnson, "Based on King's recent activities and public utterances, it is clear that he is an instrument in the hands of subversive forces seeking to undermine our nation."[14]

But King felt that he must campaign against the war. In January he had flown to Jamaica for some weeks of seclusion and writing. On the way he picked up a few magazines, and at the airport restaurant he looked at "The Children of Vietnam," an article in *Ramparts* that displayed color photographs of napalm victims. King pushed away his plate and told his aide Bernard Lee, "Nothing will ever taste any good for me until I do everything I can to end that war."[15] King felt that the rights of African Americans and of Vietnamese children were linked, that he could not speak up for one without speaking up for the other. Fired by an expanding sense of responsibility that had been sparked by his receipt of the Nobel Peace Prize, he believed that campaigns for justice and peace must be global. His reasons were pragmatic as well as moral, for he knew that the money being used to wage the war would be far better spent on the black poor and all the poor of the United States. His Riverside speech referred to the Chicago campaign and the urban riots:

> My third reason grows out of my experience in the ghettos of the North over the last three years—especially the last three summers. As I have walked among the desperate, rejected, and angry young men, I have told them that molotov cocktails and rifles would not solve their problems. . . . But they asked, what about Vietnam? They asked if our nation wasn't using massive doses of violence to solve its problems, to bring about the changes it wanted. Their question hit home, and I knew that I could never again raise

my voice against the violence of the oppressed in the ghettos without having first spoken clearly to the greatest purveyor of violence in the world today—my own government.[16]

To the end King continued to speak out against the Vietnam War and to actively support numerous antiwar initiatives.

With Vietnam and the ghettos burning, King felt a new urgency to achieve real change. No longer was there time to offer a menu of social reforms and coax the white power structure to order from it dish by dish. The popularity of politicians like George Wallace, Barry Goldwater, and Richard Nixon scared King. "They'll treat us like they did our Japanese brothers and sisters in World War II. They'll throw us into concentration camps. The Wallaces and the Birchites will take over. The sick people and the fascists will be strengthened. They'll cordon off the ghetto and issue passes for us to get in and out."[17]

King concluded that the sole solution was economic security for all Americans. This was much more radical than the "Jobs and Freedom" agenda of the March on Washington. King understood that this would be a "much harder" struggle, "a restructuring of the architecture of American society." "I am now convinced that the simplest approach will prove to be the most revolutionary—the solution to poverty is to abolish it directly by the now rather widely discussed measure—the guaranteed annual income."[18]

New goals required new strategies. What was needed was a way to dramatize American poverty and simultaneously force America to end it. In July 1967 King told an SCLC convention: "It is necessary to adopt civil disobedience. To dislocate the functioning of a city, without destroying it, can be more effective than a riot because it can be longer lasting, costly to the society, but not wantonly destructive. Moreover, it is difficult for the government to quell it by superior force."[19] That spring a young black attorney with the NAACP Legal Defense and Education Fund, Marian Wright (now Marian Wright Edelman, head of the Children's Defense Fund), had taken members of a U.S. Senate subcommittee on poverty down to Mississippi to see firsthand the devastated living conditions. In the group was Senator Robert Kennedy, whom Wright met again later that summer. When she told him she was headed down to Atlanta to meet with Dr. King, Kennedy said, "Tell him to bring the poor people to Washington." When King heard this idea, he accepted it as a revelation.

On October 23, 1967, after a summer of deadly rioting in Newark, Detroit, and dozens of other cities, King testified before the National Advisory Commission on Civil Disorders. Afterward, he told reporters that the causes of the riots were obvious, but America was not willing to change them. He spoke about the SCLC plan to organize poor people to "camp right here in Washington . . . by the thousands and thousands until the Congress of our nation and the federal government will do something to deal with the problem."[20] On October 30 King started serving a five-day sentence for violating the Birmingham injunction back in May 1963. Upon his release he told a mass meeting:

"We've got to camp in—put our tents in front of the White House. . . . We've got to make it known that until our problem is solved, America may have many, many days, but they will be full of trouble. There will be no rest, there will be no tranquility in this country until the nation comes to terms with our problem."[21]

This project, which came to be called the Poor People's Campaign, would be the SCLC's main action for 1968. Specifics were slow in developing. How many "poor people" would come? How could other groups besides blacks be included? How would they travel to Washington? How would they live? Would they demand jobs, a negative income tax, a guaranteed income? Would they block bridges, sit in at congressional offices, take over Bethesda Naval Hospital? How long could they remain? How would the police react? The kickoff date was set for April 1, then pushed back to the end of April. Plans were changing day by day.

Recruiting proved more difficult than expected. Many potential volunteers were turned off by the prospect of an indefinite stay. Others were afraid that the campaign might be taken over by violent or black-nationalist elements. These fears were encouraged by undercover FBI agents in several cities, who were directed to disrupt the campaign as much as possible. In addition to their ongoing surveillance by wiretaps and bugs, the FBI now had an informant in the SCLC leadership circle, James Harrison, who supplied the bureau with the latest campaign plans. In August the FBI had added "Black Nationalist Hate Groups"—including, for unexplained reasons, the SCLC—to their domestic "counterintelligence program" (COINTELPRO). The FBI now was officially empowered to "expose, disrupt, misdirect, discredit, or otherwise neutralize the activities of black nationalist, hate-type organizations and groupings, their leaders, spokesmen, membership and supporters, and to counter their propensity for violence and civil disorder."[22] Ironically, the new official designation did little to increase the bureau's already extensive targeting of King and the SCLC.

King felt that he was being pressured by newsmen, and after a press conference on the Poor People's Campaign, he told CBS reporter Daniel Schorr:

> I don't know if you are aware of it, but you keep driving people like me, who are nonviolent, into saying more and more militant things, and if we don't say things militantly enough for you, we don't get on the evening news. And who does? Stokely Carmichael and H. Rap Brown. By doing this, you are, first of all, selecting the more militant black leaders to be civil rights leaders, because everybody sees your television programs. And secondly, you're putting a premium on violence.[23]

Violence soon followed King to Memphis, Tennessee. On February 12, one thousand Memphis sanitation workers (almost all of whom were black) went on strike. Their wage was $1.80–$2.10 per hour, at a time when the federal minimum wage was $1.60. Two workers

SEE PAGE 229

had recently been crushed to death in a garbage packer; their benefits did not include workers' compensation. The city refused to recognize their union, and their demands were summarily rejected by Mayor Henry Loeb. A longtime segregationist, Loeb told the workers that their strike was illegal and vowed to replace them if they did not return to work. The strikers marched and held mass meetings. An umbrella organization of the Memphis black community, Community on the Move for Equality (COME), eventually decided to ask King for help.

On March 28 King led a march of five thousand on city hall. When youths at the rear of the march began to break windows and loot stores on Beale Street, police charged in, leaving one dead and sixty-two wounded. King was rushed from the scene, extremely disturbed by the violence. The FBI ordered an immediate undercover investigation of his involvement in the ill-fated march, with a view to using the information to undermine the Poor People's Campaign. King accurately anticipated severe criticism. The *New York Times* of March 31 called the Beale Street incident "a powerful embarrassment to Dr. King" and editorialized, "None of the precautions he and his aides are taking to keep the capital demonstration peaceful can provide any dependable insurance against another eruption of the kind that rocked Memphis." King scheduled a second, better-organized Memphis march for April 8.

On April 3 King was back in Memphis to address a mass meeting at Mason Temple. His flight that morning had been delayed by a bomb threat, and King recounted in his speech an earlier attempt on his life, when a deranged racist had plunged a letter opener into his chest while he was signing books in a Harlem department store in 1960. He recalled the surgeon's remarking that the blade was so perilously close to his aorta that if King had sneezed he might have drowned in his own blood. He quoted a letter he had received from a ninth grader at White Plains (New York) High School, "I'm simply writing you to say I'm so happy that you didn't sneeze." King continued:

SEE PAGE 230

> And I want to say tonight, I want to say that I am happy that I didn't sneeze. Because if I had sneezed, I wouldn't have been around here in 1960 when students all over the South began sitting-in at lunch counters. And I knew that as they were sitting in they were really standing up for the best part of the American dream. And taking the whole nation back to those great wells of democracy which were dug deep by the Founding Fathers in the Declaration of Independence and the Constitution. If I had sneezed, I wouldn't have been around in 1962, when Negroes in Albany, Georgia, decided to straighten their backs up. And whenever men and women straighten their backs up, they are going somewhere, because a man can't ride your back unless it is bent. If I had sneezed, I wouldn't have been there in 1963, when the black people of Birmingham, Alabama, aroused the conscience of this nation, and brought into being the Civil Rights Bill. If I had sneezed, I wouldn't have had the chance later that year, in August, to try to tell America about a dream that I had had. If I had sneezed, I

wouldn't have been down in Selma, Alabama, to see the great movement there. If I had sneezed, I wouldn't have been in Memphis to see a community rally around those brothers and sisters who are suffering. I'm so happy that I didn't sneeze. . . .

Well, I don't know what will happen now. We've got some difficult days ahead. But it doesn't matter with me now. Because I've been to the mountaintop. . . . And I've seen the promised land. I may not get there with you. But I want you to know tonight that we as a people will get to the promised land. And I'm happy tonight. I'm not worried about anything. I'm not fearing any man. Mine eyes have seen the glory of the coming of the Lord.[24]

After the speech, emerging from many months of depression, King was elated, as relaxed as he'd been in a long time. He hung out all night with his brother, A. D., and other friends in their rooms at the Lorraine Motel and didn't arise until noon. He waited for Andrew Young to report back from a court hearing on the upcoming march. When Young finally showed up, King "immediately started fussing in a kind of joking way about 'why don't you call and let me know what's going on? We're sitting here all day long waiting to hear from you and you didn't call'—and he picked up a pillow and threw it at me. And I threw it back, and we ended up with five or six of us in a pillow fight. . . . Occasionally he would get in those kind of hilarious moods.[25]

Around six the entourage at the Lorraine began to dress for dinner. They had been invited for soul food at the home of Rev. Billy Kyles, who came in to hurry King along. Kyles watched as King changed to a shirt with a bigger collar, and teased him about getting fat. King stepped out on the motel balcony to greet some of the party, then turned back to his room to grab a jacket.

A single bullet pierced King's jaw and neck; within minutes he was dead. Ralph Abernathy heard Andrew Young saying "Oh God. Oh God, Ralph. It is over." Abernathy gave an angry reply, "Don't you say that Andy. Don't you say that. It is not over."[26]

IN BALTIMORE DURING THE RIOTING AFTER KING'S
MURDER, APRIL 1968. **MICHAEL SULLIVAN**

The assassination of Martin Luther King, Jr., triggered riots
in over one hundred U.S. cities. The rioting left forty-six
dead nationwide, all but five of them black. It was the most
concentrated racial violence in U.S. history.

BELOW: DR. BENJAMIN SPOCK (LEFT) AND MARTIN
LUTHER KING, JR., LEADING THE "SPRING MOBE"
ANTIWAR MARCH TO THE UNITED NATIONS, APRIL 15,
1967. **BENEDICT J. FERNANDEZ**

Behind King, on the right, is James Orange of the SCLC; to
the right of King is Monsignor Rice of Pittsburgh. In his
address to the rally King said, "Everyone has a duty to
be in both the civil rights and the peace movements." The
idea of a King-Spock presidential ticket in 1968 had considerable backing from the Left but was rejected by King.

OPPOSITE: ANTI-INTEGRATION PROTESTERS, CHICAGO
SUBURB, SEPTEMBER 1966. **BENEDICT J. FERNANDEZ**

SANITATION WORKERS ASSEMBLING FOR A SOLIDARITY
MARCH, MEMPHIS, MARCH 28, 1968. **ERNEST WITHERS**

The assembly point was Clayborn Temple AME Church,
adjacent to the office of Rev. H. Ralph Jackson, an officer
of the international AME Church and chairman of Community on the Move for Equality (COME). He explained the
placards: "With those men, when you say [union] 'recognition,' that means 'We are being recognized.' This is why
they wore the sign 'I AM A MAN.'"

Ernest Withers—the Memphis-based photographer
who covered the civil rights movement in depth, starting
with the Emmett Till case in 1955—remembers helping to
cut the sticks for these signs.

SCLC LEADERS HOSEA WILLIAMS, JESSE JACKSON,
MARTIN LUTHER KING, JR., AND RALPH ABERNATHY
ON THE BALCONY OF THE LORRAINE HOTEL, MEMPHIS,
APRIL 3, 1968—THE DAY BEFORE JAMES EARLE RAY
ASSASSINATED KING ON THE SAME BALCONY.
ASSOCIATED PRESS

AFTER KING'S ASSASSINATION, AIDES POINT TO THE
SOURCE OF THE GUNSHOTS, APRIL 4, 1968.
JOSEPH LOUW

ABOVE: KING'S CHILDREN VIEWING HIS BODY LYING IN
STATE, ATLANTA, APRIL 6, 1968. **BENEDICT J. FERNANDEZ**

King's body was moved to Atlanta, where it lay in state at
Sisters' Chapel, Spelman College. Yolanda King is pic-
tured at center, with Berenice below and Martin Luther
King III to the right; the man to the left is unidentified.
Not in the picture is King's other son, Dexter Scott.

OPPOSITE: CORETTA SCOTT KING AT HER HUSBAND'S
FUNERAL, EBENEZER BAPTIST CHURCH, ATLANTA,
APRIL 9, 1968. **ASSOCIATED PRESS**

ABOVE: YOUTH RESPONDING TO NEWS OF KING'S
MURDER, HARLEM, APRIL 4, 1968. **BEUFORD SMITH**

OPPOSITE: AT THE MEMORIAL MARCH FOR KING,
MEMPHIS, APRIL 8, 1968. **ROBERT SENGSTACKE**

BELOW: RESURRECTION CITY, DURING THE POOR
PEOPLE'S CAMPAIGN, WASHINGTON, D.C., APRIL–MAY
1968. **ROBERT HOUSTON**

Resurrection City was pitched near the Lincoln Memorial,
where it remained a site of protest and dialogue for almost
two months. It was disbanded only after multiple arrests
and a mobilization of the National Guard.

OPPOSITE: MULE TRAIN, PART OF THE POOR PEOPLE'S
MARCH ON WASHINGTON, APRIL 1968. **ERNEST WITHERS**

In December 1967 Martin Luther King had officially announced his plan to march on Washington, D.C., with an
army of poor people of all races. Despite King's assassination,
the Poor People's Campaign took place as intended.

King described his plan for the Poor People's Campaign:

The only real revolutionary, people say, is a man who has
nothing to lose. There are millions of people in this country who have very little, or even nothing, to lose. If they
can be helped to take action together, they will do so
with a freedom and a power that will be a new and unset-
tling force in our complacent national life.

Notes and Sources

Introduction: "Imprisoned in a Luminous Glare"

1. Martin Luther King, Jr., *Why We Can't Wait* (New York: New American Library, 1964), p. 39.
2. Wofford, in Aldon Morris, "A Man Prepared for the Times: A Sociological Analysis of the Leadership of Martin Luther King, Jr.," in Peter J. Albert and Ronald Hoffman, eds., *We Shall Overcome* (New York: Da Capo Press, 1990), p. 45. Hereafter cited as *We Shall Overcome*.
3. Nicholas Natanson, *The Black Image in the New Deal* (Knoxville: University of Tennessee Press, 1992), chap. 4.
4. Chivers, in Cornel West, "The Religious Foundations of the Thought of Martin Luther King, Jr.," in *We Shall Overcome*, p. 123.
5. Diggs, in Clayborne Carson, David J. Garrow, Vincent Harding, and Darlene Clark Hine, eds., *Eyes on the Prize: A Reader and Guide* (New York: Penguin Books, 1987), p. 49. Hereafter cited as *Prize: A Reader*.
6. Ladner, in Stephen J. Whitfield, *A Death in the Delta* (Baltimore and London: Johns Hopkins University Press, 1988), p. 91.
7. Moody, ibid., p. 92.
8. Ibid., pp. 88–89. See also Clenora Hudson-Weems, *Emmett Till: The Sacrificial Lamb of the Civil Rights Movement* (Troy, Mich.: Bedford Publishers, 1994), pp. 85–87.
9. Moore, in Charles Moore and Michael Durham, *Powerful Days: The Civil Rights Photography of Charles Moore* (New York: Stewart, Tabori & Chang, 1991), p. 25.
10. Howard Zinn, *SNCC: The New Abolitionists* (Boston: Beacon Press, 1964), pp. 7–8. Hereafter cited as *SNCC*.
11. Warren Hinkle and David Welsh, "Five Battles of Selma," *Ramparts* 4 (June 1965): 36.
12. David Garrow, *Protest at Selma: Martin Luther King and the Voting Rights Act of 1965* (New Haven, Conn., and London: Yale University Press, 1978), p. 160. Hereafter cited as *Protest at Selma*.
13. James Martin, in Charles E. Fager, *Selma, 1965: The March That Changed the South* (Boston: Beacon Press, 1985), p. 51. Hereafter cited as *Selma*.
14. Taylor Branch, *Parting the Waters: America in the King Years, 1954–63* (New York: Simon and Schuster, 1988), p. 395. Hereafter cited as *Parting the Waters*.
15. Bond, in Howell Raines, *My Soul Is Rested* (New York: Penguin Books, 1983), p. 213. Hereafter cited as *My Soul Is Rested*.
16. Mary King, *Freedom Song: A Personal Story of the 1960s Civil Rights Movement* (New York: William Morrow, 1987), p. 215.
17. Ibid.
18. Pat Watters, *Down to Now: Reflections on the Southern Civil Rights Movement* (New York: Pantheon, 1971), p. 70.
19. Danny Lyon, "Ain't Gonna Let Nobody Turn Me Round: Use and Misuse of the Southern Civil Rights Movement," *Aperture* 115 (summer 1989): 75.
20. Cornel West, *Race Matters* (Boston: Beacon Press, 1993), p. 6.
21. U.S. Bureau of the Census, *Statistical Abstract of the United States: 1994* (Washington, D.C.: Department of Commerce, 1994).
22. Ralph Ellison, *Invisible Man* (New York: Vintage Books, 1990), p. xx.

1 The Montgomery Bus Boycott, 1955: "My Soul Is Rested"

1. Parks, in *Prize: A Reader*, p. 66.
2. Quoted in *Parting the Waters*, p. 129.
3. Nixon, interview in *Eyes on the Prize: America's Civil Rights Years, 1954–65*, part 2 (PBS, 1987), videocassette series. Hereafter cited as *Eyes on the Prize* video.
4. Parks, in *Parting the Waters*, p. 131.
5. Juan Williams, *Eyes on the Prize: America's Civil Rights Years, 1954–65* (New York: Viking Press, 1987), p. 68. Hereafter cited as Williams, *Eyes on the Prize*.
6. Nixon, in *Parting the Waters*, p. 133.
7. Nixon, in *My Soul Is Rested*, p. 45.
8. Ibid.
9. Robinson, in Peter B. Levy, *Documentary History of the Modern Civil Rights Movement* (New York: Greenwood Press, 1992), p. 56. Hereafter cited as *Documentary History*.
10. Martin Luther King, Jr., *Stride toward Freedom: The Montgomery Story* (New York: Harper and Brothers, 1958), pp. 53–54. Hereafter cited as *Stride*.
11. Ibid.
12. Nixon, in *My Soul Is Rested*, p. 49.
13. King, in *Parting the Waters*, p. 136.
14. King, in *Prize: A Reader*, p. 43.
15. Abernathy, in Williams, *Eyes on the Prize*, p. 76.
16. Crenshaw and King, in King, *Stride*, pp. 112, 113.
17. Sellers, in *Parting the Waters*, p. 150.
18. King, *Stride*, p. 128.
19. Ibid., p. 129.
20. Pollard, in *Parting the Waters*, p. 164.
21. King, *Stride*, p. 165.

22. Smiley, ibid.
23. King, *Stride*, p. 166.
24. Ibid., p. 160.
25. Ibid., pp. 164 and 169.
26. Robinson, in Henry Hampton and Steven Fayer, *Voices of Freedom: An Oral History of the Civil Rights Movement from the 1950s Through the 1980s* (New York: Bantam Books, 1991), p. 32. Hereafter cited as *Voices of Freedom*.

2 Little Rock Central High, 1957, and the University of Mississippi, 1962: "Don't Let Them See You Cry"

1. King, in George M. Houser, "Freedom's Struggle Crosses Oceans and Mountains: Martin Luther King, Jr., and the Liberation Struggles in Africa and America," in *We Shall Overcome*, p. 186.
2. Eastland, in Rhoda Lois Blumberg, *Civil Rights: The 1960s Freedom Struggle* (Boston: Twayne Publishers, 1984), p. 56.
3. Faubus, in Melba Patillo Beals, *Warriors Don't Cry: A Searing Memoir of the Battle to Integrate Little Rock's Central High* (New York: Washington Square Press, 1994), p. 38. Hereafter cited as *Warriors Don't Cry*.
4. Quoted ibid., p. 39.
5. Eckford, in *Documentary History*, pp. 45–46.
6. Quoted in Williams, *Eyes on the Prize*, p. 105.
7. Fine, in Anthony Lewis, *Portrait of a Decade: The Second American Revolution* (New York: Random House, 1964), pp. 51–52.
8. Patillo, in *Voices of Freedom*, p. 45.
9. *Warriors Don't Cry*, pp. 115–16.
10. Ibid., p. 127.
11. Eisenhower, in *Documentary History*, pp. 46–47.
12. Green, in *Voices of Freedom*, p. 48.
13. Green, in Ellen Levine, ed., *Freedom's Children: Young Civil Rights Activists Tell Their Own Story* (New York: Avon Books, 1994), p. 53.
14. Meredith, in *Documentary History*, p. 49.
15. Barnett, in Williams, *Eyes on the Prize*, p. 215.
16. Kennedy, in *Parting the Waters*, p. 659.
17. *Parting the Waters*, p. 665.
18. King, ibid., p. 672.

3 Sit-Ins and Freedom Rides, 1960–62: "This Was the Answer"

1. McCain, in *My Soul Is Rested*, p. 76.
2. Lewis, in *SNCC*, pp. 19–20.
3. Lewis, in *Parting the Waters*, p. 279.
4. Bayard Rustin, "Jail vs. Bail," *Student Voice* 1 (August 1960): 4.
5. Vivian, interview in *Eyes on the Prize* video, part 3.
6. *Prize: A Reader*, pp. 138–39.

7. *Parting the Waters*, p. 302.
8. Fox, in Robert Weisbrot, *Freedom Bound: A History of America's Civil Rights Movement* (New York: Plume, 1991), p. 20. Hereafter cited as *Freedom Bound*.
9. *Greensboro Daily News*, in Howard Sitkoff, *The Struggle for Black Equality, 1954–1980* (New York: Hill and Wang, 1981), p. 88. Hereafter cited as *Struggle for Black Equality*.
10. *Richmond News Leader*, in *SNCC*, p. 27.
11. Weisbrot, *Freedom Bound*, p. 19.
12. Sellers, in *Struggle for Black Equality*, p. 86.
13. Moses, in Clayborne Carson, *In Struggle: SNCC and the Black Awakening of the 1960s* (Cambridge, Mass.: Harvard University Press, 1981), p. 17. Hereafter cited as *SNCC and the Black Awakening*.
14. Shuttlesworth, in *Parting the Waters*, p. 273.
15. Aldon D. Morris, *The Origins of the Civil Rights Movement: Black Communities Organizing for Change* (New York: Free Press, 1984), p. 140. Hereafter cited as *Origins of the Civil Rights Movement*.
16. Farmer, in *Prize: A Reader*, p. 147.
17. *Parting the Waters*, p. 412.
18. Nash, ibid., p. 430.
19. *Prize: A Reader*, p. 159.
20. Farmer and Abernathy, in *Freedom Bound*, p. 60.

4 The Birmingham Movement, 1963: "I Don't Mind Being Bitten by a Dog"

1. Sydney Smyer, in *Parting the Waters*, p. 426.
2. Wyatt Tee Walker, "The Meaning of Birmingham," in *The SCLC Story in Words and Pictures* (Atlanta: SCLC, 1964), p. 31.
3. Shuttlesworth, in *Origins of the Civil Rights Movement*, p. 251.
4. Reagon, ibid., p. 245.
5. King, in *Prize: A Reader*, p. 172. A competing theory is that Robert Kennedy and FBI Director J. Edgar Hoover engineered the bailout; see *Origins of the Civil Rights Movement*, p. 247.
6. Pritchett, in ibid., p. 174.
7. King, in *Parting the Waters*, p. 632.
8. King, in *Origins of the Civil Rights Movement*, p. 251.
9. Reagon, ibid., p. 256.
10. Marrisett, in *My Soul Is Rested*, p. 149.
11. Bevel, in *Origins of the Civil Rights Movement*, p. 260.
12. King, ibid., p. 264.
13. Bevel, in *Eyes on the Prize*, p. 189.
14. Martin Luther King, Jr., *Why We Can't Wait* (New York: New American Library, 1964), pp. 97–98.
15. Ruth R. Hemphill, letter, *Washington Post*, May 16, 1963; in Garrow, *Protest at Selma*, p. 168.
16. The words "Rodney King" have a similar effect today.
17. *Washington Post*, in Garrow, *Protest at Selma*, p. 142.

18. Malcolm X, in William Strickland, *Malcolm X: Make It Plain* (New York: Viking Press, 1994), p. 156.
19. King, in *Parting the Waters*, p. 763.
20. King, in *Sing for Freedom: Civil Rights Movement Songs* (Washington, D.C.: Smithsonian Institution; Folkways Records, 1990), cut 20.
21. Connor, in *Freedom Bound*, p. 71.
22. Shuttlesworth, in *Parting the Waters*, p. 790.
23. Carson and Shelton, in *Prize: A Reader*, pp. 193–94.
24. King, telegraph to Kennedy, in *Parting the Waters*, p. 824.
25. President Kennedy, in *Documentary History*, pp. 118–19; and *Prize: A Reader*, pp. 120–21.

5 The March on Washington, 1963: "We Stood on a Height"

1. King, in *Parting the Waters*, p. 816.
2. The prints were designed by Lou LoMonaco and published by the Urban League.
3. Most of the facts and figures in this chapter come from Thomas Gentile, *March on Washington: August 28, 1963* (Washington, D.C.: New Day Publications, 1983), and *Parting the Waters*, chaps. 21–23.
4. Kennedy, in *Struggle for Black Equality*, p. 160.
5. Signs are quoted from photographs in the Black Star archives.
6. Young, transcribed from *I Have a Dream: The Rev. Dr. Martin Luther King, Jr., 1929–68* (New York: ABC Records, n.d.), side B, cut 3.
7. Lewis, in *Prize: A Reader*, p. 123.
8. Lerone Bennet, in Doris E. Saunders, ed., *The Day They Marched* (Chicago: Johnson Publishing, 1963), p. 12.
9. King, ibid., p. 85.
10. Gentile, *March on Washington*, p. 250.
11. Clayborne Carson, "Reconstructing the King Legacy: Scholars and National Myths," in *We Shall Overcome*, p. 240.
12. Baker, in Anthony Lewis, *Portrait of a Decade: The Second American Revolution* (New York: Random House, 1964), pp. 254–55.

6 SNCC and Mississippi, 1960–64: "A Tremor in the Middle of the Iceberg"

1. U.S. Bureau of Census figures, in Doug McAdam, *Freedom Summer* (New York and Oxford: Oxford University Press, 1988), p. 25.
2. Evers, in Williams, *Eyes on the Prize*, p. 208.
3. Noble, in *SNCC and the Black Awakening*, p. 78.
4. Moses, in *Documentary History*, pp. 94–95.
5. Moses, in *SNCC and the Black Awakening*, pp. 78–79.
6. Moses, in *SNCC*, p. 84.
7. Block, in James Forman, *The Making of Black Revolutionaries* (New York: Macmillan, 1972), p. 283. Hereafter cited as *Making of Black Revolutionaries*.
8. Peacock, in *SNCC and the Black Awakening*, p. 78.
9. *Making of Black Revolutionaries*, p. 294.
10. Moses, in *SNCC*, pp. 88–89.
11. Branton, in *Parting the Waters*, p. 718.
12. *Parting the Waters*, p. 718.
13. Lewis, in *Prize: A Reader*, p. 123. Some southern states required voters to prove they had a sixth-grade education.
14. Lowenstein, in *SNCC and the Black Awakening*, p. 97.
15. Donaldson, in *Making of Black Revolutionaries*, p. 356.
16. Barry, in *SNCC and the Black Awakening*, p. 100.
17. Moses, in Sally Belfrage, *Freedom Summer* (Charlottesville and London: University Press of Virginia, 1990), p. 9.
18. Barnett, in William Bradford Huie, *Three Lives for Mississippi* (New York: WCCBooks, 1964), p. 103.
19. Ed Pitt, ibid., p. 56.
20. Spain, "Mississippi Autopsy," in *Mississippi Eyewitness* (New York: Layman's Press, 1964), p. 49. Other reliable sources believe that Chaney's bones were broken during burial or excavation; see Seth Cagin and Philip Dray, *We Are Not Afraid* (New York: Macmillan, 1988), p. 407.
21. Huie, *Three Lives*, pp. 168–70.
22. Sellers, in McAdam, *Freedom Summer*, p. 96.
23. Sellers, in *Struggle for Black Equality*, p. 185.
24. See McAdam, *Freedom Summer*, chap. 4.
25. Savio, in McAdam, *Freedom Summer*, pp. 168–69.
26. Mary Rothschild, ibid., p. 177.
27. Chude Pamela (Parker) Allen, ibid., p. 184.

7 Selma, 1965: "We Must Go to Montgomery and See the King"

1. *Selma*, p. 72.
2. B. Lafayette, in *Making of Black Revolutionaries*, p. 319.
3. King, in *Selma*, pp. 9–10.
4. Baker, in *My Soul Is Rested*, p. 197.
5. Ibid., p. 200.
6. Baker, in *Selma*, p. 67.
7. Vivian, in Williams, *Eyes on the Prize*, p. 264.
8. Vivian may have been punched not by Clark but by a deputy; see David J. Garrow, *Bearing the Cross: Martin Luther King, Jr., and the Southern Christian Leadership Conference* (New York: Vintage Books, 1988), p. 391. Hereafter cited as *Bearing the Cross*.
9. Valeriani, in *Voices of Freedom*, p. 223.
10. Turner, in *My Soul Is Rested*, p. 189.
11. Bevel, in *Selma*, p. 83.
12. Lewis, in *My Soul Is Rested*, p. 207.
13. *Prize: A Reader*, p. 269.

14. Roy Reed, *New York Times*, March 8, 1965, p. 1; in *Protest at Selma*, p. 75.
15. Lewis, in *My Soul Is Rested*, p. 207.
16. Webb, ibid., p. 211.
17. Willie Bolden, ibid., p. 210.
18. Dr. Albert Moldovan, phone interview with author, New York, August 11, 1995.
19. Lewis, in *My Soul Is Rested*, p. 211.
20. George B. Leonard, "Midnight Plane to Alabama," *Nation*, May 10, 1965, pp. 502–5; in *Prize: A Reader*, p. 160.
21. Reese, in *Voices of Freedom*, p. 229.
22. King, in *Selma*, p. 98.
23. Moldovan, in Leonard, *Nation*; in *Prize: A Reader*, p. 162.
24. Berrigan, in "Selma and Sharpeville," *Commonweal* (April 1965): 71–75; in Levy, *Documentary History*, pp. 157–58.
25. Johnson, address before a Joint Session of Congress, March 15, 1965; in Levy, *Documentary History*, pp. 159–62.
26. Vivian, in *Voices of Freedom*, p. 236.
27. Lewis, ibid., p. 237.
28. Steele, in *Selma*, p. 155.
29. King, in James Melvin Washington, ed., *A Testament of Hope: The Essential Writings of Martin Luther King, Jr.* (New York: Harper-Collins Publishers, 1991), p. 230; with additions transcribed from *Eyes on the Prize* video, part 6.
30. Lowery, in *My Soul Is Rested*, pp. 223–24.
31. *Protest at Selma*, pp. 19, 200.
32. Webb, in *Voices of Freedom*, p. 240.

8 Black Power and the March Against Fear, 1966: "The Oppressed Against the Oppressor"

1. Lewis, in *SNCC and the Black Awakening*, p. 101.
2. Lewis, in *Voices of Freedom*, p. 206.
3. Malcolm X, in *Selma*, p. 58.
4. Malcolm X, in *Struggle for Black Equality*, p. 212.
5. Julius Lester, *Look Out, Whitey! Black Power's Gon' Get Your Mama!* (New York: Grove Press, 1968), p. 91. Hereafter cited as *Look Out*.
6. Newton and Seale, in *Voices of Freedom*, pp. 352–53.
7. *Look Out*, p. 3.
8. McKissick, in August Meier and Elliott Rudwick, *CORE: A Study in the Civil Rights Movement, 1942–1968* (Urbana: University of Illinois Press, 1975), p. 414.
9. Carmichael, in *Voices of Freedom*, p. 280.
10. Ibid., p. 289.
11. Carmichael, in *SNCC and the Black Awakening*, pp. 209–10; and in *Eyes on the Prize* II video, part 1.
12. Carmichael, in *SNCC and the Black Awakening*, p. 211.
13. King, in *Bearing the Cross*, p. 489.
14. Ibid., p. 483.
15. McKissick, in *Struggle for Black Equality*, p. 215.
16. Meredith, in Alvin F. Poussaint, "A Negro Psychiatrist Explains the Negro Psyche," in August Meier, John Bracey, Jr., and Elliott Rudwick, *Black Protest in the Sixties* (New York: Markus Wiener Publishing, 1991), p. 138.

9 The Eclipsing of Nonviolence, 1965–68: "It Is Not Over"

1. King, in *Bearing the Cross*, pp. 439–40.
2. Ibid., p. 581.
3. James L. Sundquist, *Politics and Policy—The Eisenhower, Kennedy, and Johnson Years* (Washington, D.C.: Brookings Institute, 1968), p. 281; in *Protest at Selma*, p. 295.
4. Bruce L. R. Smith, "The Politics of Protest: How Effective Is Violence?" *Proceedings of the Academy of Political Science* 29 (March 1968): 115–33; in *Protest at Selma*, p. 165.
5. King, in Adam Fairclough, *To Redeem the Soul of America: The Southern Christian Leadership Conference and Martin Luther King, Jr.* (Athens: University of Georgia Press, 1987), p. 275.
6. King, in *Bearing the Cross*, p. 444.
7. Ibid., p. 492.
8. Young, in *Voices of Freedom*, pp. 312–13.
9. King, in *Freedom Bound*, p. 183.
10. King, in *Bearing the Cross*, p. 524.
11. Martin Luther King, Jr., "Testament of Hope," *Playboy* 16 (January 1969); in Vincent Harding, "Commentary," in *We Shall Overcome*, p. 161.
12. Martin Luther King, Jr., "A Time to Break Silence," in James Melvin Washington, ed., *A Testament of Hope: The Essential Writings of Martin Luther King, Jr.* (New York: HarperCollins Publishers, 1991), p. 241.
13. Rowan, in *Documentary History*, p. 207.
14. Hoover, in *Bearing the Cross*, p. 554.
15. King, ibid., p. 543.
16. King, in *Documentary History*, p. 208.
17. Ibid., p. 596.
18. Ibid., pp. 539–40.
19. Ibid., p. 574.
20. King, in Fairclough, *To Redeem the Soul of America*, p. 357.
21. King, in *Bearing the Cross*, p. 580.
22. David J. Garrow, *The FBI and Martin Luther King, Jr.* (New York: Penguin Books, 1981), p. 182.
23. King, in *Voices of Freedom*, p. 457.
24. Martin Luther King, Jr., "I See the Promised Land," in Washington, ed., *Testament*, p. 286.
25. Young, in *Bearing the Cross*, p. 623.
26. *Voices of Freedom*, p. 467.

Sources for Quotations in the Captions

Page 19. Parks, in Martin Bush, *The Photographs of Gordon Parks* (Wichita, Kans.: Wichita State University, 1983), p. 38.

Page 22. Stephen J. Whitfield, *A Death in the Delta* (Baltimore and London: Johns Hopkins University Press, 1988), pp. 20, 39.

Page 26. Weiner's notebooks, in *Dan Weiner, 1919–1959* (New York: Grossman, 1974), unpaginated.

Page 28. Smith, in Ben Maddow, *Let Truth Be the Prejudice: W. Eugene Smith: His Life and Photographs* (New York: Aperture, 1985), p. 44.

Page 52. *Warriors Don't Cry*, p. 83.

Page 61. Elizabeth Huckaby, *Crisis at Central High* (Baton Rouge and London: Louisiana State University Press, 1980), p. 44.

Page 62. Charles Moore and Michael Durham, *Powerful Days: The Civil Rights Photography of Charles Moore* (New York: Stewart, Tabori & Chang, 1991), p. 16.

Page 68. Anne Moody, *Coming of Age in Mississippi* (New York: Dell, 1968), p. 267.

Page 76. *Making of Black Revolutionaries*, pp. 190–91.

Page 78. Lawson and Baldwin, in *Struggle for Black Equality*, p. 83.

Page 81. Danny Lyon, *Memories of the Southern Civil Rights Movement* (Chapel Hill and London: University of North Carolina Press, 1992), pp. 30, 128, 129. Hereafter cited as *Memories*.

Page 85. Ibid., p. 126.

Page 90. Rodino, in *Protest at Selma*, p. 169.

Page 104. Wrenn, interview by author, Birmingham, July 24, 1995.

Page 113. Bryant, interview by author, Birmingham, July 24, 1995.

Page 122. Baldwin, in Thomas Gentile, *March on Washington: August 28, 1963* (Washington, D.C.: New Day Publications, 1983), p. 252.

Page 124. Nat Herz, unpublished manuscript, pp. 1 and 22.

Page 128. *Parting the Waters*, p. 889.

Page 130. Brock, in Vicki L. Crawford, Jacqueline Anne Rouse, and Barbara Woods, eds., *Women in the Civil Rights Movement: Trailblazers and Torchbearers, 1941–1965* (Bloomington and Indianapolis: Indiana University Press, 1993), p. 124.

Page 131. *Memories*, p. 136.

Page 144. Forscher, phone interview by author, August 14, 1995.

Page 147. *Memories*, p. 110.

Page 148. John Dittmer, *Local People: The Struggle for Civil Rights in Mississippi* (Urbana and Chicago: University of Illinois Press, 1994), p. 204.

Page 149. Varela, letter to author, January 1996.

Page 150. Parker, in Douglas McAdam, *Freedom Summer* (New York and Oxford: Oxford University Press, 1988), p. 86.

Page 154. Dennis, in *Eyes on the Prize*, p. 240.

Page 154. Moses, in William Bradford Huie, *Three Lives for Mississippi* (New York: WCCBooks, 1964), p. 232.

Page 157. *Look Out*, p. 27.

Page 158. Sally Belfrage, *Freedom Summer* (Charlottesville and London: University Press of Virginia, 1990), pp. 245–46.

Page 160. *Bearing the Cross*, p. 358.

Page 180. Amelia Boynton Robinson, *Bridge across Jordan* (Washington, D.C.: Schiller Institute, 1991), pp. 255–56.

Page 181. Forman, in *SNCC and the Black Awakening*, p. 160. Clemson, in Moore and Durham, *Powerful Days*, p. 170.

Page 183. Christopher Wren, "Turning Point for the Church," *Look*, May 18, 1965, p. 32.

Page 185. Orsini, ibid., p. 37.

Page 191. Reading, letter to author, November 1995.

Page 202. *Parting the Waters*, p. 320.

Page 202. Mitchell, phone interview by author, August 14, 1995.

Page 204. Roberts, in William Strickland, *Malcolm X: Make It Plain* (New York: Viking Press, 1994), p. 202.

Page 211. Reading, letter to author, November 1995.

Page 213. All quotes from Dittmer, *Local People*, pp. 399–400.

Page 214. Parks, in Bush, *Photographs of Gordon Parks*, p. 42.

Chronology of the Civil Rights Movement, 1954–68

1954 | **May 17** In *Oliver Brown et al. v. Board of Education of Topeka, Kansas,* the U.S. Supreme Court rules that segregated schools are unconstitutional.

July 11 First White Citizens Council is formed in Indianola, Mississippi.

1955 | **August 28** Emmett Till, a Chicago youth visiting relatives in the South, is lynched in Money, Mississippi, after he flirts with a white shopkeeper.

September 21–23 Till's uncle, Moses Wright, is the first black to testify against a white in a Mississippi murder trial. The murderers are acquitted.

December 1 Rosa Parks is arrested in Montgomery, Alabama, for violating segregation laws on a city bus.

December 5 A black boycott of Montgomery buses begins. Rev. Martin Luther King, Jr., is elected to lead the Montgomery Improvement Association (MIA).

1956 | **February–March** Autherine Lucy is the first black student to attend the University of Alabama. After white students riot, she is expelled.

March 12 The Southern Manifesto condemning the *Brown v. Board* decision is signed by 102 southern members of the U.S. Congress.

June 11 The National Association for the Advancement of Colored People (NAACP) is banned in Alabama. In Birmingham the Alabama Christian Movement for Human Rights (ACMHR) is founded, with Rev. Fred Shuttlesworth as president.

November 13 The Supreme Court rules that Montgomery buses must be integrated.

December 21 Montgomery buses are integrated; the boycott ends.

1957 | **January 10–11** The Southern Christian Leadership Conference (SCLC) emerges from an Atlanta meeting of southern civil rights leaders, mostly ministers. King becomes its president.

August 29 The Civil Rights Act of 1957 is passed. It sets up a civil rights commission and strengthens the U.S. Justice Department's authority in voting rights violations.

September The Little Rock Nine seek to enter Little Rock Central High School but are kept out by rioting whites. President Dwight D. Eisenhower sends in the National Guard to enforce the school's integration.

1960 | **February 1** Four black college students ask for service at a whites-only F. W. Woolworth's lunch counter in Greensboro, North Carolina, sparking the sit-in movement, which rapidly spreads to all the southern states.

February–May Nashville students stage the biggest, best-organized sit-in demonstrations and eventually win legal integration of lunch counters throughout the city.

April 15–17 The Temporary Student Nonviolent Coordinating Committee (later SNCC) is established at an SCLC meeting in Raleigh, North Carolina.

October 19–27 Jailed for an Atlanta sit-in, King is aided by presidential candidate John F. Kennedy; King's support for Kennedy is a factor in his election.

1961 | **May 4** The first "Freedom Riders" leave Washington, D.C., aboard two buses in an attempt to desegregate southern bus terminals.

May 14 Freedom Riders are beaten by mobs outside Anniston, Alabama, and at the Anniston and Birmingham Trailways terminals.

May 20 Freedom Riders are beaten by a mob at a Montgomery bus terminal. Federal marshals are sent in.

May 24–26 Freedom Riders travel from Montgomery to Jackson, Mississippi, escorted by National Guardsmen. In Jackson they are arrested and sent to jail.

July In McComb, Mississippi, near the Louisiana border, Robert Moses establishes the first SNCC voter-registration outpost, a model for future efforts.

August Albany, Georgia, is chosen by a SNCC national conference to be the site of an intensive antidiscrimination and voting rights drive.

November The first demonstrations are held in Albany, Georgia. A coalition of black organizations, the Albany Movement, is formed.

1962 | September When James Meredith attempts to become the first black to study at the University of Mississippi, rioting ensues, eventually quashed by federal troops. Meredith attends his first class on October 1.

1963 | April 3 Project C is launched in Birmingham. A comprehensive attack on the city's discriminatory practices, it is meant to have national repercussions.

April 12 King is arrested in Birmingham for violating an injunction against demonstrations.

May 2–7 Phase III of Project C puts thousands of trained protesters on Birmingham's streets. The Commissioner of Public Safety, Bull Connor, stages brutal attacks with police dogs and water cannons, which become an international scandal.

May 10 After King and Shuttlesworth announce an accord with white city leaders in Birmingham, King's motel room is bombed; black rioting ensues.

June 11 Governor George Wallace stages his "stand in the schoolhouse door," an unsuccessful gesture to block integration of the University of Alabama at Tuscaloosa. President Kennedy makes an impassioned televised civil rights speech.

June 12 Mississippi NAACP leader Medgar Evers is murdered outside his Jackson home by Byron de la Beckwith, who is not convicted until his third trial, in 1994.

August 28 The March on Washington brings 200,000–500,000 demonstrators together for the biggest protest assembly in the United States to date.

September 15 Four black schoolgirls are murdered in the dynamiting of the Sixteenth Street Baptist Church in Birmingham.

1964 | June The Mississippi Freedom Summer Project brings hundreds of volunteers into the state to aid voter-registration campaigns and set up "freedom schools."

June 21 Three Freedom Summer workers are murdered in Neshoba County, Mississippi. Attorney General Robert Kennedy and President Lyndon B. Johnson order an intensive search for their bodies and their assailants.

July 2 The Civil Rights Act of 1964 is passed, outlawing discrimination in voting, public accommodations, and employment.

August 4 The bodies of the three murdered civil rights workers are found. Twenty men, some of them police, are eventually charged with conspiracy to murder James Chaney, Andrew Goodman, and Michael Schwerner; seven are convicted.

August 22–26 The Democratic National Convention in Atlantic City is attended by delegates of the Mississippi Freedom Democratic Party (MFDP), who attempt to replace the all-white regular delegation. After Fannie Lou Hamer's televised speech, President Johnson proposes a compromise seating, which is rejected by the MFDP.

December 10 King is awarded the Nobel Peace Prize.

1965 | January–February A full-scale voter-registration drive begins in Selma, Alabama. Hundreds of demonstrators are arrested by Sheriff Jim Clark.

February 18 In Marion, near Selma, protester Jimmie Lee Jackson is shot dead by a state trooper.

February 21 Malcolm X is assassinated by Black Muslim hitmen at the Audubon Ballroom in Harlem.

March 7 On "Bloody Sunday" the first Selma march is beaten back at Edmund Pettus Bridge by state troopers and Sheriff Clark's deputies. The nation is outraged by photographs and film of the attack. Washington responds by expediting voting rights legislation. King calls for clergymen from across the nation to join a second march.

March 9 On "Turnaround Tuesday," King leads the second Selma march over the Pettus Bridge and then right back to Selma. That evening Rev. James Reeb is clubbed to death.

March 21–25 Under the protection of a federalized National Guard, the Selma to Montgomery march proceeds to the state capitol, where a rally of 50,000 people is held.

August 6 The Voting Rights Act of 1965 is signed into law. It bans voter examinations and provides for federal registrars to be sent to recalcitrant counties. It prompts a huge rise in black registration.

August 11–16 Rioting breaks out in the Los Angeles ghetto of Watts, the most devastating racial uprising in the United States to date.

1966 | **January** The SCLC joins a campaign for better housing and schooling in Chicago.

June 6–26 James Meredith is wounded by a sniper on the second day of his solo March Against Fear. Leaders of SNCC, CORE, and the SCLC continue the 220-mile march from Memphis to Jackson. The notion of "Black Power" comes to prominence.

July 10 King leads a large march to Chicago's city hall.

July 12–15 As rioting breaks out in Chicago, King negotiates with Mayor Richard Daley.

August Marchers in outlying Chicago neighborhoods are attacked by "White Power" mobs. A compromise accord is signed by black leaders and white politicians.

October The Black Panther Party for Self-Defense is founded by Huey Newton and Bobby Seale in Oakland, California.

1967 | **April 4** King condemns the U.S. war in Vietnam in a speech at New York's Riverside Church.

July Large-scale rioting in Newark, Detroit, and other cities. The worst outbreak of urban rebellions in U.S. history leaves scores dead, hundreds wounded, thousands arrested, and millions of dollars' worth of property destroyed.

August 25 FBI director J. Edgar Hoover officially targets civil rights groups for his Counterintelligence Program (COINTELPRO) of surveillance and neutralization.

December 4 King announces his plan to bring thousands of poor people of all races to Washington, D.C., to press for jobs and income.

1968 | **March 28** King leads a march in support of striking sanitation workers in Memphis. After youths at the rear of the march turn violent, King vows to return for another, more peaceful march.

April 4 King is assassinated by a white sniper on the balcony of the Lorraine Motel in Memphis. Black rioting erupts in more than one hundred cities.

April–June Led by the new head of the SCLC, Ralph Abernathy, the Poor People's Campaign erects Resurrection City near the Lincoln Memorial in Washington, D.C. About twenty-five hundred protesters—mostly African American, Hispanic, and Native American—take up residence in tents and shacks. They demonstrate to little effect; the last of the demonstrators are evicted by the police and the National Guard on June 24.

Acknowledgments

First gratitude goes to all the photographers who contributed their pictures to this book. Many photographers also gave generously of their knowledge: Ida Berman, Tommy Giles, John Goodwin, Joe Holloway, Jr., Julius Lester, Spider Martin, Francis Mitchell, Robert Sengstacke, Bill Strode, and Tamio Wakayama. Bob Fletcher and Matt Herron were especially helpful. James Karales, Charles Moore, Charmian Reading, Maria Varela, and Ernest Withers have been both important sources of information and warm friends.

I am most grateful to Myrlie Evers-Williams, Chair of the NAACP, for her impassioned foreword, and to Jan Harris-Temple for facilitating.

For interviews, thanks to Danella Bryant, Howard Chapnick, Marty Forscher, Charlotte Billups Jernigan, Paul Jones, Jimmie Laxon, Marilyn Lowen, Elizabeth Sutherland Martinez, Dr. Al Moldovan, Tommy Wrenn, and Dorothy Miller Zellner.

For help in obtaining pictures, I would like to thank: Rickie Louise Brunner at the Alabama State Archives; Patricia Lantis, Yvette Reyes, and Gulnara Samoilova at the Associated Press; Brian Heatherington and Norma Stevens at the Avedon Studio; Marvin Whiting at the Birmingham Public Library; Voncell Williams at the *Birmingham News;* Yakiko Launois, Esther Mercado, Enid Sandri, and Eric Williams at Black Star; Debra Goodsight and Sarah Partridge at Corbis/Bettmann; Nancy Carrizales and Tom Keller at Magnum; Lynn Williamson at the *Montgomery Advertiser;* Tony Decaneas at Panopticon, Inc.; and Guy Arello, Joanna Fiore, Winifred Haun, and Sandra Weiner.

Additional help came from friends and colleagues: Maurice Berger, Townsend Davis, Sean Devlin, Ellen Dugan of the High Museum of Art, Steve and Glenda Jo Orel, Robert and Joyce Menschel, Mary Panzer of the National Portrait Gallery, Mary Yearwood of the Schomburg Center, Sam Walker at the National Voting Rights Museum and Institute in Selma, and Harry Weintraub.

At Abbeville, Robert Abrams, Nancy Grubb, Celia Fuller, and Laura Straus were wonderful.

This book would not have been made without the support of Ben Chapnick of Black Star and Howard Greenberg of the Howard Greenberg Gallery.

Selected Bibliography

Albert, Peter J., and Ronald Hoffman, eds. *We Shall Overcome.* New York: Da Capo Press, 1990.

Bailey, Ronald W., and Michèle Furst, eds. *Let Us March On! Selected Civil Rights Photographs of Ernest C. Withers, 1955–1968.* Boston: Massachusetts College of Art, 1992.

Beals, Melba Patillo. *Warriors Don't Cry: A Searing Memoir of the Battle to Integrate Little Rock's Central High.* New York: Washington Square Press, 1994.

Belfrage, Sally. *Freedom Summer.* Charlottesville and London: University Press of Virginia, 1990.

Blumberg, Rhoda Lois. *Civil Rights: The 1960s Freedom Struggle.* Boston: Twayne Publishers, 1984.

Branch, Taylor. *Parting the Waters: America in the King Years, 1954–63.* New York: Simon and Schuster, 1988.

Breines, Wini. *Community and Organization in the New Left: 1962–1968.* South Hadley, Mass.: J. F. Bergin Publishers, 1982.

Bullard, Sara, ed. *Free at Last: A History of the Civil Rights Movement and Those Who Died in the Struggle.* Montgomery, Ala.: Southern Poverty Law Center, 1989.

Cagin, Seth, and Philip Dray. *We Are Not Afraid.* New York: Macmillan, 1988.

Carawan, Guy, and Candie Carawan. *Sing for Freedom: The Story of the Civil Rights Movement Through Its Songs.* Bethlehem, Penn.: Sing Out Publications, 1990.

Carmichael, Stokely, and Charles Hamilton. *Black Power: The Politics of Liberation in America.* New York: Random House, 1967.

Carson, Clayborne. *In Struggle: SNCC and the Black Awakening of the 1960s.* Cambridge, Mass.: Harvard University Press, 1981.

Carson, Clayborne, David J. Garrow, Vincent Harding, and Darlene Clark Hine, eds. *Eyes on the Prize: A Reader and Guide.* New York: Penguin Books, 1987.

Crawford, Vicki L., Jacqueline Anne Rouse, and Barbara Woods, eds. *Women in the Civil Rights Movement: Trailblazers and Torchbearers, 1941–1965.* Bloomington and Indianapolis: Indiana University Press, 1993.

Davis, Thulani. *Malcolm X: The Great Photographs.* New York: Stewart, Tabori & Chang, 1993.

Dittmer, John. *Local People: The Struggle for Civil Rights in Mississippi.* Urbana and Chicago: University of Illinois Press, 1994.

Evans, Sara. *Personal Politics: The Roots of the Women's Liberation Movement in the Civil Rights Movement and the New Left.* New York: Knopf, 1979.

Fager, Charles E. *Selma, 1965: The March That Changed the South.* Boston: Beacon Press, 1985.

Fairclough, Adam. *To Redeem the Soul of America: The Southern Christian Leadership Conference and Martin Luther King, Jr.* Athens: University of Georgia Press, 1987.

Forman, James. *The Making of Black Revolutionaries.* New York: Macmillan, 1972.

Garrow, David J. *Protest at Selma: Martin Luther King and the Voting Rights Act of 1965.* New Haven, Conn., and London: Yale University Press, 1978.

————. *The FBI and Martin Luther King, Jr.* New York: Penguin Books, 1981.

————. *Bearing the Cross: Martin Luther King, Jr., and the Southern Christian Leadership Conference.* New York: Vintage Books, 1988.

Gitlin, Todd. *The Sixties: Years of Hope, Days of Rage.* New York: Bantam, 1989.

Hampton, Henry, and Steven Fayer. *Voices of Freedom: An Oral History of the Civil Rights Movement from the 1950s Through the 1980s.* New York: Bantam Books, 1991.

Hansberry, Lorraine. *The Movement: Documentary of a Struggle for Equality.* New York: Simon and Schuster, 1964.

Harding, Vincent. *Hope and History: Why We Must Share the History of the Movement.* Maryknoll, N.Y.: Orbis Books, 1990.

King, Jr., Martin Luther. *Stride toward Freedom: The Montgomery Story.* New York: Harper and Brothers, 1958.

————. *Why We Can't Wait.* New York: New American Library, 1964.

————. *A Testament of Hope: The Essential Writings of Martin Luther King, Jr.* Edited by James Melvin Washington. New York: HarperCollins Publishers, 1991.

King, Mary. *Freedom Song: A Personal Story of the 1960s Civil Rights Movement.* New York: William Morrow, 1987.

Kluger, Richard. *Simple Justice: The History of Brown v. the Board of Education and Black America's Struggle for Equality.* New York: Knopf, 1976.

Lester, Julius. *Look Out, Whitey! Black Power's Gon' Get Your Mama!* New York: Grove Press, 1968.

Levine, Ellen, ed. *Freedom's Children: Young Civil Rights Activists Tell Their Own Story.* New York: Avon Books, 1994.

Levy, Peter B. *Documentary History of the Modern Civil Rights Movement.* New York: Greenwood Press, 1992.

Lewis, Anthony. *Portrait of a Decade: The Second American Revolution.* New York: Random House, 1964.

Lewis, David L. *King: A Critical Biography*. New York: Praeger, 1970.

Lyon, Danny. *Memories of the Southern Civil Rights Movement*. Chapel Hill: University of North Carolina Press, 1992.

Manning, Marable. *Race, Reform, and Rebellion: The Second Reconstruction in Black America from 1945 to 1982*. Jackson: University Press of Mississippi, 1984.

McAdam, Doug. *Freedom Summer*. New York: Oxford University Press, 1988.

Meier, August, and Elliott Rudwick. *CORE: A Study in the Civil Rights Movement, 1942–1968*. Urbana: University of Illinois Press, 1975.

Meier, August, John Bracey, Jr., and Elliott Rudwick, eds. *Black Protest in the Sixties*. New York: Markus Wiener Publishing, 1991.

Mills, Kay. *This Little Light of Mine: The Life of Fannie Lou Hamer*. New York: Dutton, 1993.

Moody, Anne. *Coming of Age in Mississippi*. New York: Dell, 1968.

Moore, Charles, and Michael Durham. *Powerful Days: The Civil Rights Photography of Charles Moore*. New York: Stewart, Tabori & Chang, 1991.

Morris, Aldon D. *The Origins of the Civil Rights Movement: Black Communities Organizing for Change* (New York: Free Press, 1984).

Murray, Paul T. *The Civil Rights Movement: References and Resources*. New York: G. K. Hall, 1993.

Powledge, Fred. *Free at Last? The Civil Rights Movement and the People Who Made It*. Boston: Little, Brown, 1991.

Raines, Howell. *My Soul Is Rested*. New York: Penguin Books, 1983.

Robinson, Jo Ann Gibson. *The Montgomery Bus Boycott and the Women Who Started It*. Knoxville: University of Tennessee Press, 1987.

Seeger, Pete, and Bob Reiser. *Everybody Says Freedom*. New York: W. W. Norton, 1989.

Sitkoff, Howard. *The Struggle for Black Equality, 1954–1980*. New York: Hill and Wang, 1981.

Strickland, William. *Malcolm X: Make It Plain*. New York: Viking Press, 1994.

Wallace, Michele. *Black Macho and the Myth of the Superwoman*. New York: Warner Books, 1980.

Weisbrot, Robert. *Freedom Bound: A History of America's Civil Rights Movement*. New York: Plume, 1991.

West, Cornel. *Race Matters*. Boston: Beacon Press, 1993.

Williams, Juan. *Eyes on the Prize: America's Civil Rights Years, 1954–65*. New York: Viking Press, 1987.

Zinn, Howard. *SNCC: The New Abolitionists*. Boston: Beacon Press, 1964.

Recordings and Videos

Eyes on the Prize, Part I—America's Civil Rights Years: 1954 to 1965. A Six-Part Series. Produced by Blackside, Inc., 1990. Distributed by PBS Video, Arlington, Va.

Eyes on the Prize, Part II—America at the Racial Crossroads: 1964 to 1985. An Eight-Part Series. Produced by Blackside, Inc., 1990. Distributed by PBS Video, Arlington, Va.

Freedom Is a Constant Struggle: Songs of the Mississippi Civil Rights Movement. Folk Era Productions, 1994. Distributed by RM Distributing, Division of Aztec Corporation, Naperville, Ill.

Pete Seeger—We Shall Overcome: The Complete Carnegie Hall Concert, Historic Live Recording, June 8, 1963. CBS Records, 1989.

Sing for Freedom: The Story of the Civil Rights Movement Through Its Songs. Smithsonian Institution; Folkways Records, 1990. Distributed by Rounder Records, Cambridge, Mass.

Index

Photography Credits

Copyright © Bob Adelman/Magnum Photos: frontispiece, 122–23, 127, 199; Alabama Department of Archives and History: 27 (both); AP/Wide World Photos: 21, 41, 46, 67, 89, 175, 202, 230, 233; copyright © Eve Arnold/Magnum Photos: 79; copyright © Richard Avedon, courtesy Richard Avedon: 29, 144; copyright © George Ballis/Take Stock: 154 (right), 158; copyright © Ida Berman: 39, 40; copyright © *Birmingham News*. All rights reserved. Reprinted by permission: 105; Chicago Defender: 22; copyright © Bruce Davidson/Magnum Photos: 87, 103 (top), 187, 188–89, 190 (bottom); copyright © Elliott Erwitt/Magnum Photos: 9; copyright © Benedict J. Fernandez, courtesy Howard Greenberg Gallery: 226, 227, 232; copyright © Bob Fitch/Black Star: 212; copyright © Bob Fletcher: 147, 159; copyright © Leonard Freed/Magnum Photos: 125, 161; copyright © Burt Glinn/Magnum Photos: 61, 217; Bob Gomel/Life Magazine, copyright © Time Inc.: 201; copyright © Ernst Haas/Magnum Photos: 101; copyright © Declan Haun, courtesy Howard Greenberg Gallery: 77, 174; copyright © Matt Herron/Take Stock, courtesy Howard Greenberg Gallery: 148, 150, 213, 214; copyright © Estate of Nat Herz, courtesy Barbara Singer: 115, 124; copyright © Robert Houston/Black Star: 236; Carl Iwasaki/Life Magazine, copyright © Time Inc.: 59; copyright © James Karales, courtesy Howard Greenberg Gallery: 163, 182–83, 184 (right); copyright © Hiroji Kubota/Magnum Photos: 193; copyright © John Loengard: 113; Joseph Louw/Life Magazine, copyright © Time Inc.: 231; copyright © Danny Lyon/Magnum Photos: 80, 81, 82, 85, 99, 128, 129, 131, 145, 146; copyright © Spider Martin: 177, 178, 179, 180 (both), 186; copyright © Ivan Massar/Black Star: front cover; copyright © Vernon Merritt III/Black Star: 208, 209; copyright © Francis Hamlin Mitchell: 203; copyright © Charles Moore/Black Star, courtesy Howard Greenberg Gallery: 28, 47, 48 (both), 49, 62, 64 (both), 65, 83, 102, 103 (bottom), 104, 106, 107, 108 (both), 109, 110, 111, 176, 181 (all); copyright © Gordon Parks, courtesy Howard Greenberg Gallery: 19, 24–25, 215; copyright © Charmian Reading, courtesy Howard Greenberg Gallery: 191, 210, 211; copyright © Bill Reed/Black Star: 156; copyright © Steve Schapiro/Black Star: 153, 184 (left), 185 (bottom), back cover; copyright © Robert A. Sengstacke: 206, 235; copyright © Beuford Smith: 234; copyright © Bill Strode/Black Star: 185 (top); copyright © Michael Sullivan/Black Star: 225; Kenneth Thompson, copyright © General Board of Global Ministries, courtesy Howard Greenberg Gallery: 100, 133, 157; UPI/Corbis-Bettmann: 20, 23, 51, 60, 63, 78, 86 (top and bottom), 112, 126, 152, 154 (left), 160, 190 (top), 200, 204, 205; copyright © Maria Varela: 149, 207; copyright © Tamio Wakayama, courtesy Howard Greenberg Gallery: 151, 155; copyright © Fred Ward/Black Star: 130; copyright © Sandra Weiner: 26, 42, 43, 44, 45; copyright © Ernest Withers, courtesy Panopticon Gallery: 31, 84, 228–29, 237.

For Gulnara and Talia

FRONT COVER: ON THE SELMA TO MONTGOMERY MARCH, MARCH 21–25, 1965.
IVAN MASSAR. Martin Luther King, Jr., is at the center, in the white cap. Next to him on the right is Coretta Scott King; on her right is John Lewis, chairman of SNCC.

BACK COVER: SUMMER PROJECT VOLUNTEERS SINGING "WE SHALL OVERCOME," THE ANTHEM OF THE CIVIL RIGHTS MOVEMENT, JUNE 19, 1964. STEVE SCHAPIRO. The volunteers are departing for Mississippi after completing their training sessions in Oxford, Ohio.

FRONTISPIECE: THE MARCH ON WASHINGTON FOR JOBS AND FREEDOM: THE CROWD GATHERING AT THE WASHINGTON MONUMENT, AUGUST 28, 1963 (DETAIL). BOB ADELMAN. See pages 122–23.

PICTURE EDITOR: STEVEN KASHER
EDITOR: NANCY GRUBB
DESIGNER: CELIA FULLER
PRODUCTION EDITOR: OWEN DUGAN
PRODUCTION MANAGER: RICHARD THOMAS

First edition
10 9 8 7 6 5 4 3 2 1

Library of Congress Cataloging-in-Publication Data
Kasher, Steven.
    The civil rights movement : a photographic history, 1954–68 / Steven Kasher.
        p.   cm.
    Includes bibliographical references and index.
    ISBN 0-7892-0123-2
    1. Afro-Americans—Civil rights—History—20th century—Pictorial works.
2. Civil rights movements—United States—History—20th century—
Pictorial works. I. Title.
E185.61.K347   1996
323.1'196073'00222—dc20   96-4337